Without Regrets
A Study of Ecclesiastes

Second Edition

Kristi Burchfiel

Without Regrets: A Study of Ecclesiastes
Copyright © 2018, 2009 by Kristi Burchfiel. All rights reserved.

No part of this publication may be reproduced, stored in a retrieval system or transmitted in any way by any means, electronic, mechanical, photocopy, recording or otherwise without the prior permission of the author except as provided by USA copyright law.

Published in the United States of America

ISBN: 9780692960141

All Bible translations are taken from the New American Standard Version.

Reviews

I have known Kristi Burchfiel for several years. I am not surprised at her ability to discern the depth of the word of God. She has taken the book of Ecclesiastes and made its truth come to life. You will be encouraged and will move toward a life "Without Regrets" as a result of Kristi's work.

Dr. Ted Kersh
Former Pastor
South Tulsa Baptist Church, Tulsa, Oklahoma

Kristi Burchfiel's study of Ecclesiastes is an excellent, practical book on how to relate the truths found in Solomon's writing to daily life. I highly recommend this book for an individual or group Bible study. She has gleaned the very heart of the book of Ecclesiastes in a way that will make it come alive. It is well written and organized for simplicity while she is able to present the profound truths found in it.

The study is written in a way that individuals can use it for their personal devotion and work through the scriptures to bring insight into their personal relations with the Lord.

A church would be blessed to use this book as a Sunday School study or to be used in a cell group.

Pat Bullock
Associate Pastor - Summit Church, Corpus Christi, TX
Former Director of Missions, Heart of Kansas Southern Baptist Association

Kristi takes the much-discussed and often-quoted words of Ecclesiastes and cleverly provides down-to-earth, relevant questions and suggestions to help transform how to go about your daily living. This study works equally well for an individual or group. I thoroughly enjoyed delving into Without Regrets.

Chris Crowe
Lifegroup Leader
LifeChurch.tv, Edmond, Oklahoma

Acknowledgments

Many thanks to Chris Crowe for holding me accountable and reviewing during the writing process. She did a fantastic job helping me make sure my sometimes random ideas made sense.

Thanks also to the Summit Church Ladies' Sunday School class in Wichita, Kansas, for graciously being willing to spend their Sunday mornings going through an unknown study and providing their invaluable feedback.

Thanks to my family for their patience and encouragement, as I've spent so much time and energy focused on completing this endeavor.

Finally, thanks to my Heavenly Father for his infinite patience and guidance and for continuing to prod me to complete this enormous undertaking. May God be glorified in this, my act of obedience.

Kristi Burchfiel

Table of Contents

REVIEWS	3
ACKNOWLEDGMENTS	5
TABLE OF CONTENTS	7
FOREWORD TO SECOND EDITION	11
INTRODUCTION	13
SESSION 1: WITHOUT REGRETS	**15**
Why Study Ecclesiastes?	16
Solomon: The Author	18
The Author's People (Audience)	20
Conclusion	21
Discussion Questions	21
SESSION 2: EVERYTHING IS MEANINGLESS	**23**
Solomon's Thesis	24
Solomon's Examples	25
Solomon's Reasons	26
Solomon's Qualifications	26
Conclusion	28

| DISCUSSION QUESTIONS 30

SESSION 3: SOLOMON'S EXPERIMENTS 31
    SOLOMON'S EXPERIMENTS 32
    CONCLUSION 38
    DISCUSSION QUESTIONS 40

SESSION 4: TIME AND JUSTICE 41
    SOLOMON'S OBSERVATIONS: TIME..42
    SOLOMON'S OBSERVATIONS: JUSTICE 44
    CONCLUSION 46
    DISCUSSION QUESTIONS 47

SESSION 5: POWER AND ATTITUDE 49
    SOLOMON'S OBSERVATIONS: POWER 49
    SOLOMON'S OBSERVATIONS: ATTITUDE 53
    CONCLUSION 56
    DISCUSSION QUESTIONS 56

SESSION 6: LIFE 59
    SOLOMON'S OBSERVATIONS: LIFE 59
    CONCLUSION 63
    DISCUSSION QUESTIONS 64

SESSION 7: DESCRIBING WISDOM 65
    IT IS BETTER TO HAVE WISDOM THAN FOLLY. 66
    CONCLUSION 71
    DISCUSSION QUESTIONS 71

SESSION 8: APPLYING WISDOM TO LIFE 73
    IT IS BETTER TO HAVE WISDOM THAN FOLLY. 73
    CONCLUSION 79
    DISCUSSION QUESTIONS 81

SESSION 9: LIVING TO DIE 83
    WE WILL ALL DIE SOMEDAY 83
    CONCLUSION 88
    DISCUSSION QUESTIONS 89

SESSION 10: THE FOOL AND HIS REWARD 91
    FOOLISHNESS IS DETRIMENTAL TO ALL..92
    CONCLUSION 97
    DISCUSSION QUESTIONS 98

SESSION 11: ATTITUDE ADJUSTMENT 99
- ATTITUDE TOWARD OTHERS 100
- ATTITUDE TOWARD THE FUTURE 102
- ATTITUDE TOWARD WORK 104
- ATTITUDE TOWARD LIFE 106
- CONCLUSION 109
- DISCUSSION QUESTIONS 109

SESSION 12: ENHANCE YOUR MEMORY 111
- REMEMBER YOUR PAST 112
- REMEMBER YOUR FUTURE 114
- REMEMBER TRUTH 116
- REMEMBER GOD 118
- CONCLUSION 120
- MY MEMORIAL 121
- DISCUSSION QUESTIONS 123

LEADER'S GUIDE 125
- LEADING A SMALL GROUP 126
- SESSION KEY FOCUS POINTS 129

BOOK OF ECCLESIASTES OUTLINE 133

ABOUT THE AUTHOR 139
- OTHER BOOKS 140

HOW TO BECOME A CHRISTIAN 141

Kristi Burchfiel

Foreword to Second Edition

When I first published Without Regrets in 2009, it was my first time publishing anything and I had no idea what I was doing and no concept of where it would lead me. In the 9 years since taking that first step in this journey, I have been amazed and surprised and humbled at the response. I've learned many things about myself, about the publishing world, and about how interesting God's will can become when we are willing to take one step at a time down the path He leads us on. Since this time, many individuals, small groups, and churches have let me know how much this study has helped them and given them great focus on what God has for their lives. To God be the glory!

I have been thinking about the possibility of a second edition for some time, but not until my original publisher went through bankruptcy and the book went out of print in early 2017 did I put anything into action. Faced with the book no longer being available, I began to put together what is now this second edition. In addition to reviewing and revising the content of the book, I've also added discussion questions at the end of each session and a brief Leader's Guide at the end to aid in small group discussions or in personal self-reflection.

Living through regrets is a difficult and limiting way to live and deprives us of the opportunity to experience all that God wants to do in and through us. It is my continuing prayer that as you read through and study Ecclesiastes, you will be challenged to not make the same mistakes that Solomon did and to keep your focus on God and His will for your life. Only as we follow Him will we be able to truly know what it means to live Without Regrets.

Introduction

"I glorified You on earth, having accomplished the work which You have given me to do."

These words, spoken by Jesus and recorded in John 17:4, sum up the entire life and works of Jesus. He did everything the Father had for Him to do. As Jesus prayed that prayer in the garden of Gethsemane the night before His death, He was able to look back over His life here on earth. He saw many things He could have done but didn't. After all, there were several more people He could have healed, countless more sermons He could have preached, and thousands of towns He never set foot in. However, He was able to look back on His life and say, "I did everything I was given to do by my Father. I have no regrets."

So then, when we look back on our life thus far, what do we see? Do we have situations in our past we wish we would have done differently? Some of these changes might be inconsequential when we look at our life as a whole, such as, "I wish I would have studied French." These types of regrets are minor and usually have little to no guilt or remorse attached to them. On the other hand, some of the changes might be more profound, such as, "I wish I had never cheated on my spouse," or "If only I had been a better witness for Christ while in college." These types of regrets can result in lots of guilt and shame and have lasting consequences. God, in His grace and mercy, forgives us our shortcomings and makes us new. The question becomes, "How do we avoid having additional regrets from this point forward?"

This study takes us through the book of Ecclesiastes. In this book, we will learn from the experiences, observations, and advice that Solomon, king of Israel, gleaned from his own life. Solomon, with all his wisdom, also had a great many regrets. He offers this book as encouragement to us to learn from his mistakes.

What does it take to live a life without regrets? Join me as we explore that question further in the sessions to come.

Session 1: Without Regrets

Regrets. Many people don't think about them until after they are actually experiencing them. We live today in such a fast-paced world that it can be difficult to stop and reflect on our decisions before we make them. The effects of how we choose to live our lives impact many people besides just ourselves. Since we can't go back and change actions or words that occurred in the past, it is important to understand what leads us to actions that result in regret. If we can identify ways to avoid those actions, we can avoid a lot of regret down the road. This brings us to the book of Ecclesiastes.

Ecclesiastes is not typically the most studied book in the Bible. I've attended church my entire life and can remember only hearing a couple of sermons or messages preached from this book. Some of you may have read a chapter or two on your own at some point or read through it as part of a Bible reading plan. While I was studying Ecclesiastes, I started asking friends of mine from both religious and non-religious backgrounds what they had heard about the book or what they thought about it. I heard a wide array of responses including depressing, pointless, boring, or not relevant in today's world. After spending time studying the book, I find it extremely relevant to today's life and I agree with preacher and author John Philips, who has described the book of Ecclesiastes in his messages and commentaries as the book of Solomon's regrets.

Why Study Ecclesiastes?

The theme of Ecclesiastes is pretty straightforward: making much of nothing, striving after wind, earnestly seeking after something that vanishes in thin air. What a picture of disappointment The second verse into the book states that "Everything is meaninglessness." So if everything is meaningless, why bother delving further into the book? There are several reasons that you and I should study the book of Ecclesiastes. I'll list the three main ones that I discovered while studying it.

1. It's in the Bible. Every book of the Bible is inspired by God and is His very words to us (2 Timothy 3:16). This fact alone makes the book worthy of study.

2. It's written as a warning. We'll get into this later on, but this book is designed to be a warning to people so that others do not fall into the same temptations as the writer.

3. The truths are relevant to today's world. Again, we'll see this in more detail later, but the truths discussed throughout the book are ones that still are debated by people in general.

My study of the book of Ecclesiastes began after a time of personal struggle. I had been a follower of Jesus Christ for many years and had become, in a sense, a little overconfident in my own faith in Christ. It can be easy in this culture to say that we are a Christian and have faith in Christ, but then spend all our time doing for ourselves without really feeling it necessary to trust in Christ. In this culture especially, we pride ourselves on being able to "pull ourselves up by our own bootstraps." However, this attitude of self-reliance is neither biblical nor Christ-like.

My struggle reached a critical point when faced with some difficult circumstances in my personal life. I realized I was willing to compromise in an area I had never thought I would even be tempted. Things I knew were wrong began to be easily justified as a means to an end. My thoughts ran along these lines: Surely God won't mind if I do just a little bit of this. After all, it's not that big of a deal, and the end result may help me in the long run. Thankfully, I came to the point where I actually listened to what I was saying to myself and realized what a potentially dangerous situation I had put myself in. I started to run through in my mind some of the things I had been telling myself that had led to the edge of such a slippery slope. I discovered, much to my surprise, that I had my own self-pleasure in mind, not God's plan. I realized a profound truth: I can't trust myself to know or do what is best for me.

That is when my crisis hit. If I can't trust myself, how am I supposed to make the necessary day-to-day decisions? How do I handle not being in control? How do I avoid landing myself in situations guaranteed to create feelings of guilt and regret later? What do I do now? That is when God led me to the book of Ecclesiastes. Instead of just handing me the answers to my questions, God had me search through and find them for myself. This journey changed my life, and I believe God will change you through this journey as well.

As we begin to study the book of Ecclesiastes, my prayer is that, whether you are at a spiritual crossroads or not, you will search out for yourself God's truth in this book and that He will help you avoid some of the pitfalls I experienced as well as some of the pitfalls the writer of Ecclesiastes experienced.

Solomon: The Author

Solomon is generally accepted as the author of Ecclesiastes. When studying any book, it is important to study the author, if possible. Every author has a specific purpose, perspective, and people in mind when writing. We're going to spend the remainder of this session getting familiar with the background behind the writing of the book before we dive into Ecclesiastes itself.

The Author's Purpose

Most authors have a purpose in writing. Sometimes they just want to explain facts so people will have a better understanding about something. Other times, the author is trying to persuade the reader to do something, believe something, buy something, etc. Other purposes might include feeling better about himself or getting something off his chest, such as journaling. Frequently, authors have multiple purposes when writing.

Based on Ecclesiastes 1:1-2 and 12:9-14, summarize Solomon's purpose for writing Ecclesiastes. Think about your purpose for reading this book. How does it compare to Solomon's purpose for writing it?

_____

_____

_____

The Author's Perspective

Authors also have a perspective from which they are writing. Regardless of how objective a person tries to be, God has allowed each of us to experience different situations that have given us a certain perspective on life. Solomon had experienced many things throughout his life, and these events led him to write this book. Solomon was also at a specific place in history prior to the birth, death, and resurrection of Christ. Here is a listing of some of the generally accepted background information regarding Ecclesiastes.

- Principal personalities: The Preacher or Teacher, generally accepted as Solomon
- Historical Setting: Around 935 BC at the end of Solomon's life. (He died in 930 BC) Unified Kingdom of Israel
- Geography: He was king of Israel in Jerusalem
- Style: Autobiographical and instructional. Meant to be a sermon

Another important aspect in understanding a person's perspective is any life experiences the author has been through. Let's take a look at some key events in Solomon's life.

Read 1 Kings 2:1-4 and 3:1-15 and describe the major events of Solomon's early life.

_____

_____

_____

_____

Read 1 Kings 9:1-9, 10:23-25, 11:1-13, 26-43. What devastating piece of news does Solomon receive late in life? How does he respond?

_____

_____

_____

Once Solomon learns that his son will not be inheriting the kingdom that he has worked so hard to build and expand, he is overcome with anger. What's more, the kingdom will be split, and a majority is going to be given to one of Solomon's servants. Solomon is so angry that he tries to have the servant killed. In the wake of these devastating events, Solomon sits down to write Ecclesiastes.

The Author's People (Audience)

The very act of writing something down implies that it will be read at some point, either by the author or by someone else. Solomon does not name a specific person or group of people to whom he is addressing himself. However, he gives us a clue by how he identifies himself in the book.

What is the title that he uses to refer to himself (Ecclesiastes 1:1)?

_____

Based on him calling himself a preacher or teacher, who would you assume he is writing to?

_____

Most preachers have congregations that listen to them, and teachers have students. In a broader sense of the word, preaching refers to teaching others in order to help them live correctly. Many parents have preached to their wayward teenager. Preaching is done (or should be done) out of a deep love and a desire to see the recipient return or continue right living, avoid difficulty and discipline, and eliminate ignorance. However, even the most effective preaching cannot change things for a person who will not listen or heed the warnings given.

Conclusion

While there are many detailed answers to the above questions, when looking at all of them together, a statement can be made about why Solomon wrote this book. In short, Solomon wrote to all those who would listen (people), in order to instruct and entreat them (purpose) to not make the same mistakes that he made and suffer the same regrets (perspective). Certainly, this is a worthwhile goal that gives us something to look forward to in the sessions ahead.

Discussion Questions

1. As you think about the reasons that you are studying this book, discuss how you want this study to impact your life?
2. Do you have regrets? How do your regrets compare to the regrets that Solomon may have after learning about his life?
3. Do you think it is possible to live a life without regrets? Why or why not?

Session 2: Everything is Meaningless

Individualism, materialism, capitalism, and several other isms can be easily used to describe our nation today. We have become a nation of bigger, faster, higher, and we want individual credit for any idea that turns out with a positive result. We are a prideful and egocentric people. We are taught from an early age that you cannot trust others and the only way to be successful is to "pull yourself up by your own bootstraps."

Now, as Christians, we aren't exempt from this struggle. Sure, we know it's wrong to seek after these types of materialistic or egocentric things. But sometimes we become deceived as to how rooted this idea is in our daily lives. Even the humblest of Christians fight constantly against pride. But pride is not the only sin that easily ensnares us. The lust for worldly wealth, success, fame, and prosperity weighs heavily on the minds of many Christians in our materialistic society. Solomon's world was not so very different. In fact, this desire to know everything and experience things firsthand is as old as Adam and Eve. Solomon learned how pointless this desire is after spending a lifetime seeking to experience everything first hand. Now he wants us to learn the same truth from his mistakes. Solomon opens his sermon with a declaration of his understanding of the meaning of life.

Solomon's Thesis
Read Ecclesiastes 1:1-2.

When I was writing papers in school, my English teachers always spoke about the importance of having a thesis statement. That statement summarizes the entire paper into one sentence. A good thesis would be catchy, memorable, and inclusive of the main points covered in the paper. Solomon does not waste any time. He jumps right in and states his thesis right from the very beginning in verse two. Many translations use the word vanity. Using a dictionary or other Bible translations, write a definition for the word vanity.

_____

_____

_____

_____

Some of the words I came across include: *meaninglessness, futility, nothingness*. Solomon is stating that everything in life is totally and completely worthless and a waste of time.

Read Psalm 39:5-6. How does this idea, written by King David, Solomon's father, compare?

Solomon's Examples
Read Ecclesiastes 1:3-11.

List as many of the subjects as you can that Solomon refers to as being meaningless.

These nine verses include quite a list. Solomon wants to make sure that everyone understands that when he said, "All is vanity," in verse two, he meant exactly that. Working, having children, nature, trying to come up with something new, memory—they all made the list, including several others. Which ones in the list stick out to you?

Solomon knows that you are probably skeptical of his thesis. He also knows that, in order for you to trust his conclusion, you have to have some trust in him. So next, Solomon lists his reasons and his qualifications for making this claim.

Solomon's Reasons
Read Ecclesiastes 1:12-13.

Solomon was a king, and a rich king at that. Why did he want to spend his time philosophizing about the meaning of life? Why did he not just enjoy life? Why was he always searching for more? Why do we ask why so often? Reread verse 13.

We as humans cannot possibly know everything about everything in life, but that does not keep us from asking. God knew when He made us that we could not have all knowledge like Him, but He made us with minds that search question, and desire to understand all the intricacies of life. Always wondering and never knowing for certain has led many people to feel afflicted. The countless questions about why this and why that are the driving force behind many courses of study and even our professions today, such as psychology, philosophy, biology, mathematics, physics, and literature, to name a few.

So, why did Solomon want to know what in life has meaning? He was curious because God has made us all curious.

Solomon's Qualifications
Read Ecclesiastes 1:14-18.

When was the last time you got advice on what medications to take from your hairdresser? What about recommendations on steak sauce from a vegetarian? Would you trust what they told you? In both the professional world and the personal world, people can become very focused on the degrees a person can list behind their name. We want to make sure that when we follow someone else's advice, they know what they are talking about.

What qualifications would you want to see by a person's name before you trusted their assessment of the meaning of life?

___

___

___

Solomon wants to assure you that he does in fact have the necessary qualifications to make his statement about the vanity of life and have people listen to it and follow it. What does Solomon say are his qualifications in verses 16 and 17?

___

___

Now, only you can decide if his listed qualifications are going to be enough to convince you to take him seriously, but before you decide, I would add another thought. Since this book has an earthly author and a divine author, we must take into consideration the credentials of both. Solomon may have had a surplus of wealth and wisdom, but it is completely overshadowed by the Creator of wealth and wisdom. God is the author of the Bible through the Holy Spirit and He wants us to know and understand what He is saying about the meaning of life and how to live it productively, and He chose to use Solomon to convey the message.

Conclusion

A particular phrase occurs twice in this chapter and I hope you didn't miss it. It is found in verse 14 and verse 17. Write it here.

_____

Different versions say it differently, but in the New American Standard Version, it says "striving after wind." I love this word picture. Can't you just see a child running out into an open field trying to grab hold of the wind? He's running here and there with outstretched arms and hands. He quickly clinches his fists but catches hold of nothing. The Hebrew word used here for wind is *ruach*, which literally means breath, spirit, vapor. A couple of different Hebrew words are used throughout Ecclesiastes and are translated into English as striving. However, they both come from the root word *rea*, which refers to a person's purpose or aim. Basically, this phrase refers to a person who is striving after or aiming for something that is here one minute and gone the next. In this phrase is the whole of Solomon's argument. We are a people who are spending all our time, energy, and resources trying to attain something that will evaporate into thin air as soon as we grasp it.

Solomon's father, David, understood this idea. He wrote it in this way: "Man is like a mere breath; His days are like a passing shadow," (Psalm 144:4). Incidentally, the Hebrew word for breath in this verse, *hebel*, is the exact same word that is translated *vanity* in Ecclesiastes 1:2.

The question then becomes—Are we busy running in circles trying to grab onto something that always seems to slip through our fingers? Take a minute and think about the things that you feel like you are chasing such as happiness, recognition, or financial security, and list them here.

_____

_____

_____

_____

Have you ever thought you caught them? How long did they last before they were replaced by something else? Do you feel like that child running in circles? Are you looking for something substantial?

Read Psalm 18:2, and see how David describes God.

David's descriptions of a rock and a stronghold are fixed, permanent structures that do not move. We can take hold of God and know that He will not fade. If we have accepted Jesus as our Lord and Savior, He is the Rock that we can hold onto.

Are you holding on to the Rock or are you chasing the wind? Or are you desperately trying to do both? It is very difficult to hold on to a rock and chase the wind at the same time, yet many Christians are feverishly trying to do that very thing. Take some time and examine what you are trying to gain in this life. Since our lives are "mere breaths" that will soon fade, are you making the most of your time?

Over the next few sessions, we will examine some of the ways that Solomon tried to chase the wind and what he discovered about each way he tried.

Discussion Questions
1. What are some of the things you or those around you have sought after? How has that impacted your life?
2. Have you ever felt that life was meaningless? Why or why not?
3. How do you feel about Solomon's qualifications to discuss the meaning of life? How does God's authorship impact your thoughts about that?

Session 3: Solomon's Experiments

Think for a moment. Who are you? How do you define yourself? What differentiates you from everyone else in this world? What are some of your accomplishments? Take a few minutes, and write down a description of yourself.

_____

_____

_____

> People recognize themselves in their commodities; they find their soul in their automobile, hi-fi set, split-level home, kitchen equipment.
>
> Herbert Marcuse, 1898-1979;
> German political philosopher

Even though this statement was made decades ago, Marcuse's perspective only grows truer as time goes by. People continually view themselves in terms of what they have, what they do (or have done), or who they are related to. We have been so trained to view ourselves in this manner it can be difficult to describe ourselves any other way. Therefore, it seems natural that Solomon would begin his quest for the meaning of life by experimenting with his accomplishments and possessions.

Solomon's Experiments
Physical and Material Pleasure
Read Ecclesiastes 2:1-11.

Record all the different ways Solomon sought pleasure.

_____

_____

_____

To refresh your memory on Solomon and all he did in his life, you can look up 1 Kings 7:1-12, 9:15-21, 10:14-23, and 11:1-3. He's rich. He could have any material possession that entered his mind. He could have slaves build him palaces and gardens and anything else he thought he wanted. He also had a lot of women in his life—one thousand that we know of. In spite of all this, how does he describe this pursuit of pleasure (Ecclesiastes 2:11)?

_____

_____

Who doesn't want to be happy? Most of us would like to be able to enjoy life and have the things that please us. Life is more comfortable that way. Even the most devout of Christians would usually admit that if God gave them a choice, they would rather be happy than miserable. I know I would. The problem comes from seeking happiness as the goal of life. If you are constantly striving to do things just in order to fulfill whatever pleasurable thought enters your head at the moment, you will quickly learn that the feeling does not last very long. Besides, the definition of what brings happiness changes from time to time. You will be constantly searching for the next thing to impart that happy feeling. Solomon realized this. He said the whole pursuit was absolutely wasted and futile.

Think about your own life. Since the idea of success in our culture is driven by this idea of financial prosperity and "happiness," the pressure to have more stuff can be a constant. Look back at how you defined yourself earlier, including all your accomplishments. When you look at everything that is listed there, do those things by themselves make you feel fulfilled?

When Solomon realized that pleasure wasn't fulfilling, he moved on to something else.

Wisdom
Read Ecclesiastes 2:12-17.

Think about someone that you consider wise. How would you describe them?

_____

_____

Now think about someone you consider foolish. How would you describe them?

_____

_____

We've already established that Solomon had earthly wisdom. Read 1 Kings 3:5-14. Solomon was granted wisdom as a gift from God, and he had firsthand experience of how being wise while here on earth was better than being foolish. Practically speaking, life is much easier for a person who is wise. Wise people make smarter decisions with peers, with family, with education, and with money than foolish people. However...

Read Psalm 49:10.

Solomon realized that wise people are not granted immortality; they die. Solomon's response this time, unlike before when pleasure did not satisfy him, was not to just simply say, "This is vanity," and move on. When his wisdom comes up short, Solomon says that he "hated life" and that all he had done in this life was "grievous" to him (Ecclesiastes. 2:17). Why this profound despair? Imagine...

> *You wake up in the morning, and before you even open your eyes, you realize things are different. The bed you went to sleep on is not nearly so comfortable anymore. In fact, it seems kind of itchy. You feel wind whipping around and sharp pricks against your skin. It's also unbearably hot. You open your eyes and see that you are lying in the middle of a desert. You have no idea where you are and no idea how you got there, but the yellow ocean of sand extends for as far as the eye can see in every direction. You decide that you'll have to walk for it since you don't know where you are*

or if anyone is looking for you. Frantically, you realize that you don't have any water. You arbitrarily decide to go north, at least as close as you can figure based on the sun. You start walking.

You walk for what seems like hours, but the scenery doesn't change. Your skin is turning a bright red, and the sweat pours down. Your tongue is becoming thick and swollen in your mouth. Time seems to go on forever, and so does the sand. You finally get to the point where you realize that you will not survive much longer without something to drink. You press on harder, hoping to top the next hill and see an oasis. The mirages begin to play with your mind, and the desperation grows. Finally, you stumble down a hill of sand and lay at the bottom, unable to find the strength to get up. Looking up into the sun, you cry, "God, please help me!"

Next, you hear a voice. "Ask what you wish me to give to you."

You are shocked and wonder if it is your mind playing tricks on you, but the statement is repeated.

"Ask what you wish me to give to you."

Breathlessly, you whisper, "Please, God. Just a swallow of water. That is what I need most in this situation. That will help me find the strength to go on a little longer. Please..."

Then, next to where you lay, a small cup with just a swallow of water appears. You close your eyes in gratitude as you bring the water to your lips and then hold it in your mouth for the briefest of moments before you swallow.

Stop! I don't know about you, but if I'm in that situation and God asks me what I want, I'm asking Him to get me out of there. I want to go home! I've got water in the refrigerator at home—gallons of it. Just getting a little sip of water in that situation is simply prolonging the inevitable. True, my suffering was eased momentarily, and my life was temporarily improved, but that sip of water is not going to have long-lasting effects.

That's what Solomon realized. He had asked God for wisdom to govern the people, and God had granted his request. However, now he had to come to terms with the fact that being wise had only helped him in this life; it had only prolonged the inevitable fact that he would die one day. His request had helped him through some difficult times, and God had blessed him with riches as well, but he had already proven the futility of having wealth. Now he had realized that his wisdom was also futile in pursuing the meaning of life. The most amazing opportunity of requesting a gift from God had been used requesting a gift that was only temporary. He collapsed with despair.

While Solomon lay deep in his despair, he thought of all the things that he had done with his money and his wisdom. He had labored extensively throughout his kingdom. What of that?

Labor
Read Ecclesiastes 2:18-23.

Earlier, we listed all the material possessions that Solomon had. He had invested a large portion of his younger days as king creating beautiful gardens and palaces. He had so much wealth that silver was not even considered valuable in his day because of its abundance (1 Kings 10:27). However, what was he going to do with all his possessions and wealth once he died?

What is the purpose of having a "Last Will and Testament?" How do you know for certain that your wishes will be carried out?

Solomon had been granted wisdom, and he had done very well for himself. He was respected and wealthy. He made good business decisions and had prospered in every way a man could. However, as many people know, being wise yourself does not insure that your children will be wise. Once he died, Solomon would have no control over the decisions his son would make, how he spent the money, what he did to the palace, or how he governed the country. Solomon hoped that he had taught his son well. However, there had been that prophet who had come and said the kingdom would be divided and the largest portion would go to one of Solomon's servants. Solomon realized that all the work he had done would one day be nothing more than a fleeting memory recorded in some book. He realized that all this laboring had been in vain. He could not build an empire that would extend beyond him because he had no control of what happened after he died.

All of his work had been in vain. Everything Solomon had held dear had been shown to be nothing more than smoke. Remember the phrase he used in chapter one: "chasing the wind." He now truly felt that his life and been spent running around gleefully trying to capture something that simply evaporated into nothingness. He had asked for wisdom and received it plus riches. The riches had done him no lasting good, and all the things he had done with his wisdom would not extend much beyond the grave. His labor had no lasting significance. The question of the meaning of life has boiled down into a simple question for him: "What should I have asked God for?"

Glance back at 1 Kings 3:5-14. God had been pleased with what Solomon had asked. What Solomon had asked for was not a bad thing. Solomon had made a choice that was good and had served him very well throughout his life. God even gave him riches in addition to the wisdom. But what about verse 14? How does that fit in with God's gift to Solomon of wisdom?

Conclusion
Read Ecclesiastes 2:24-26.

Solomon gives us his first glimpse into his conclusion. This conclusion is reflected in a psalm he wrote. Summarize these verses from Psalm 127:1-2.

_____

_____

_____

_____

_____

The New Testament records several statements by people who had the same conclusions. Summarize what they wrote.

John – 1 John 2:15-17 _____

_____

James – James 1:17 _____

_____

Paul – Philippians 3:7-8 _____

_____

Jesus – Matthew 4:4; John 17:3 _____

_____

Solomon was beginning to understand that the most wonderful and amazing thing that a person can experience here on earth is knowing God. God gives us everything we have that is worth having. Solomon's words in verses 24-26 of chapter two are not a license to have one long party and do whatever feels good. He proved earlier that is vanity. Solomon is saying that God has given us everything worth having and we should enjoy the gifts of God in a way that pleases God. The person who continues to be pleasing in the sight of God will be given knowledge, wisdom, and joy (notice none of those things are material possessions), and the person who is not pleasing to God will end up helping the godly to gain wisdom, knowledge, and joy.

Look back at your description of yourself. One day I sat down to write a description of all the things I am and have accomplished. Instead, I came up with a much longer list of things that I am not. When I finally came down to it, I realized the only thing I can claim to be is a creation of God and, through my faith in Jesus Christ as my Lord, I am His child—nothing more, and certainly nothing less. The jobs that I do, my responsibilities, my personality, my family, my friends—these are all gifts God has graciously allowed me to have, and I must treat them as such. However, the moment I begin to think I am defined by any of those other things, I lose sight of the fact that I am created by God and I am His child; then my priorities get incorrectly shifted. I have no other claim on life and I am entitled to nothing other than what God allows me to have.

What should Solomon have asked for? He still has not said exactly, but hopefully you have an idea. Like any good scientist, he wants to explore all possibilities before coming to a final conclusion. Since all of Solomon's trials have failed, he starts to look around himself at the rest of the world to see if perhaps they know something he does not.

Discussion Questions
1. How do you describe yourself?
2. Has there been a time when you have tried various experiments to find meaning in life? What type of things did you try?
3. What is your reaction to the idea that Solomon asked for something temporary instead of something eternal? What would you have asked for?

Session 4: Time and Justice

Have you ever gone to a mall, a restaurant, or an airport and just spent time watching people? It can be fascinating. People act in many different ways in response to circumstances and situations or even culture. Being observant can be highly beneficial if you are ever in an unfamiliar circumstance. My husband and I spent some time in Spain shortly after we were married. We were not familiar with the customs or the culture, and even though I can speak the language, we were unsure of ourselves in several different situations. (Restaurants were particularly interesting!) More than once, we got the look that says "silly American" from a person who could not figure out what we were trying to do. However, we watched the other people around us and, by the end of our month-long stay, we were relatively proficient in the basic cultural areas.

Solomon realized he was in unfamiliar territory. He's still trying to figure out the answer to the question of what he should have asked God for, and nothing under his personal control could give him the answers. He decided that he would look around and see what other people do. Maybe they had found something he had overlooked. He wanted to know as much about life in general as he could, for surely increased knowledge would lead him to the meaning of life. Solomon sat back to observe.

The word *observe* is defined in a dictionary as: 1) to perceive, notice; 2) to watch attentively; 3) to make a systematic or scientific observation. I can just see Solomon sitting in his palace looking out over his kingdom or being carried by servants over the countryside and watching people. He learned many things and summed them up in five categories: time, justice, power, attitude, and life in general. We will look at the first two of these in this session.

Solomon's Observations: Time
Read Ecclesiastes 3:1-9. Record the number of occurrences of the word time.

___

Your number will depend on the translation you are using. I count thirty occurrences of the word time in these verses in the New American Standard Bible. Regardless of the translation, the word time is used a lot. When you hear the word time, what are some of the things you think of?

___

___

In thinking about this passage, I don't think Solomon is trying to expound on deep theological principles. He is simply trying to make the reader understand that many things happen in life, but there is a balance. People are being born, but they are also dying. Planting is important, but if you don't first remove the weeds that are growing in a field, your planting will not be very successful. The important idea from this is the value of moderation in what we do and of evaluation of the results. Different situations require different responses. We must realize that while some situations require us to be silent, there are also circumstances where speaking is essential. The same goes for all the items listed in these verses.

Thinking about this passage in chapter three, look back at Ecclesiastes 1:3-11. How do these two passages compare?

He still has the same conclusion. Verses 1:3 and 3:9 are practically identical. Solomon is restating his theme in different words. From the passage in chapter one, you remember, he goes on to state that man has the grievous task of being curious (1:13). Let's look at where he goes from the passage in chapter three.

Read Ecclesiastes 3:10-15. Compare verse 11 with chapter one verse 13.

God has placed in us a curiosity, but since God placed eternity in our hearts, nothing on this earth will satisfy that curiosity. God knows there is only so much that we will ever be able to understand about eternity, and we will never know all that He has done from the beginning of time through the end of time. Because of that, Solomon's conclusion is to be curious but not to the point where you are upset and worried about what has happened or what will happen (3:12). While we have a curiosity for eternal things, we can enjoy the temporal things.

Read Ecclesiastes 3:14-15.

Solomon's conclusion above may have sounded somewhat depressing to some people, and if it did, you missed the point. Ultimately, God knows and understands all things. He set everything in motion, and He gave everything its allotment of time. For us, He allowed us to be curious and to want to know more, but He also made it where nothing on earth would be able to satisfy that curiosity. Our quest to find something that satisfies only ends in peace once we have found God and His gift of salvation through His Son Jesus Christ. From that point on, the quest changes slightly as we seek to glorify God while here on this earth.

Solomon's Observations: Justice

Many of us have seen the statue of Lady Justice. She carries scales in one hand to ensure that justice is fair, a sword in the other hand to enforce justice, and she goes blindfolded to demonstrate that justice is not persuaded by any outside influence. Oh, if only it were that simple.

Solomon did some observing around his kingdom about the justice system, and his conclusions are not nearly so ideal.

Read Ecclesiastes 3:16.
How does it describe the justice of man?

_____

_____

Solomon states that wickedness is there. Any justice that man tries to give is going to be unjust. Man can try, but we are all sinful and have no right to judge one another anyway, not to mention that any judging will be influenced by our own sinful self.

Read Ecclesiastes 3:17-18.

Who has authority to judge us? When He judges us, what is the result?

_____

_____

_____

Only God has the authority to judge us, and when he sees us, He sees that we are no better than the animals, according to Solomon. This is not a favorable judgment, and Solomon sees the consequences of this judgment.

Read Ecclesiastes 3:19-22.

What is the one thing we are assured of?

_____

Death is a certainty. Solomon saw it all the time. He had never seen anyone cheat death or not have to experience it. There will be an ending to our lives here on earth. Several verses discuss this issue of finality.

Read the verses and summarize what they say about death.

Genesis 3:19 _____

_____

Psalm 49:12,20 _____

_____

Romans 6:23 _____

_____

Hebrews 9:27 _____

_____

We must realize that we all have one fate and, because of our sin, we are going to experience death. As Solomon was looking at it, it didn't matter whether someone was rich, poor, smart, foolish, man or woman—everyone was going to experience death. God then reminds us that after death, there is judgment by the One who is fully qualified and capable of judging us.

Conclusion

God has created a timetable on which all things should hinge. We may not understand the subtle nuances of that timetable, but we must respect them, realizing that God understands best. Once we have realized that, we know that we must be in constant pursuit of what God has in store for us, which is one of the results of God placing in us a desire to understand and know eternity. God knew that we would need something to search after, and He wanted it to be Him. This quest only results in peace once we have found Him and His gift of salvation through Jesus.

We also must understand that no one on earth is just or righteous by themselves, and therefore nothing that is done by men can be considered righteous. Only God is able to judge, and one day He will. In the meantime, man will continue to suffer from the same finality that God has allowed the rest of the beasts to have. But He has made provision for those who have sought after Him and found His Son to be able to continue on with Him through eternity, since they realized that He was the only thing worth seeking after in the first place.

Solomon continues His observations in the next couple of chapters, and we'll see if His conclusion holds true in other areas of life.

Discussion Questions
1. Discuss the idea of moderation. What is a situation where taking one of the ideas from the list to an extreme would not be good?
2. How do you balance curiosity so that it doesn't become worry or anxiety?
3. Give an example of a time you didn't receive what you deserved. How did you respond?

Kristi Burchfiel

Session 5: Power and Attitude

Think of someone you know whom you consider to be powerful. What type of characteristics does that person possess? How do they use their power? How did they get their power? Do you respect that person, fear that person, or avoid that person? What kind of attitude does that person have?

We can see power in many places, and so did Solomon. Solomon has continued his observations, and this session will examine not only power but attitude as well.

Solomon's Observations: Power
Oppression as a Means of Power

Read Ecclesiastes 4:1-3.

> Power tends to corrupt, and absolute power corrupts absolutely.
> John Emerich Edward Dalberg (1834–1902)

How do these verses in Ecclesiastes and this quote by John Dalberg compare?

_____

_____

_____

_____

Solomon looks out, and he sees people being oppressed by those in power. Now, this could have included himself, since he was the king. He did have a lot of slaves who were busy building all of the projects he had done in his kingdom. However, he also could have been looking in his court and at other officials. At any rate, he wrote that it was better to have not been born than to have to live under oppression.

Labor as a Means of Power
Read Ecclesiastes 4:4-8.

List some ways in which you labor.

_____

_____

_____

We all have reasons why we do the things we do: money to pay bills, enjoyment, or a sense of accomplishment. Solomon isn't necessarily saying that laboring is bad. He gives an example of what he means in verse 8.

Reread Ecclesiastes 4:8. What are the questions that the man should have asked himself.

___

___

___

We all must ask ourselves this question. Why do we labor and toil? What are we trying to accomplish? What am I giving up to be able to do this work? Many of us have heard stories about people at the end of their lives wishing they'd spent more time with family instead of working. Solomon is having some of the same thoughts now at the end of his life. First, he noticed it in his own experiences (Ecclesiastes 2:11), and now he sees that he is not alone. Many other people experience the same drive to accomplish "stuff" without taking into consideration why they are striving so hard or what they are sacrificing to accomplish it.

Friendship as a Means of Power
Read Ecclesiastes 4:9-12. How do you define friendship?

___

___

___

Having relationships with other people is an idea that God created. He desires for us to be around other people. He gave Adam Eve. David had Jonathon. All throughout the Bible, you see people having and needing friends. Could friendship ever be considered bad?

Unfortunately, people in this world use other people in a negative way. This can be included in the idea of friendship sometimes. Some people cultivate "friendships" with others solely to see what they can gain by having them as friends. Politics is one area we see this happen a lot, but it is by no means the only area. The question we must ask ourselves is, "What is our motivation for having a relationship with a certain person?" Is it for what we can get out of them? Or is it for mutual sharing and helping?

As Solomon looked around, he was seeing that two people can do more than one. Then, later, he goes on to state that three people are better than two. There is power in numbers. Having friends is very important, and we must be sure to cultivate our relationships with other people. However, we should guard our motivations for having friends.

Wisdom as a Means of Power
Read Ecclesiastes 4:13-16.

Wisdom is certainly something that Solomon can relate to. With his gift of wisdom, he had impressed a number of people throughout his lifetime. Wisdom had allowed him to rule effectively. Wisdom had helped him to govern his people. Yet, at the end, what had he said about his own wisdom? Reread Ecclesiastes 2:15.

As Solomon looked out at the world and the circumstances in the world, he began to notice something. Not all those in power are wise, and not all those who are wise are in power. However, those who have wisdom often have the capability of working situations and circumstances out to where they gain more power. Reread Ecclesiastes 4:14-16.

What happened to the wise youth who had once been in prison?

Eventually, he was made king, but Solomon states that in the end, no one will remember him. He will die and that will be the end, but while he was here and used wisdom, he was able to work his way into a powerful position.

Solomon's Observations: Attitude

I'm sure we've all heard about the importance of having a good attitude from someone at some point in our life. Our attitude toward the things that life throws our direction can influence greatly how well we cope with those situations. Solomon noticed this as well and saw two attitudes that were prevalent and are the cause of many problems for people.

Wrong Attitudes toward God
Read Ecclesiastes 5:1-7.

Our sacrifice to God is important and is mentioned in several other places in the Bible. Romans 12:1 talks about bringing ourselves as a living sacrifice. Psalm 51:17 states that the sacrifices of God are a broken and contrite heart. Here, in these verses, Solomon starts by describing the sacrifice of fools.

The sacrifice of fools has two parts. Define one part of the fool's sacrifice based on Ecclesiastes 5:2-3.

_____

_____

_____

Being rash with your mouth or uttering words hastily is considered a foolish attitude to have toward God. Why is this wrong? See the reason in Ecclesiastes 5:2.

_____

_____

The very fact that God is in heaven and I am on Earth is reason enough for me to be silent in his presence. He is God. Running to Him and babbling on incessantly is disrespecting Him of His sovereignty.

What is the second sacrifice of fools? Read Ecclesiastes 5:4-6

_____

_____

Making a vow with your mouth that you don't intend to keep or that you cannot keep is considered a foolish attitude to have toward God. What happens to us when we do not keep our vow?

_____

_____

God has never broken a vow that He has made to us. When we make a thoughtless vow to God, we must still be willing to pay the vow, for the consequences of not fulfilling a vow are far worse.

As an example, let's go back to the time in Israel's past when they were battling the inhabitants of the promised land.

Jephthah, a leader in Israel, went out to fight the Ammonites and made a foolish vow. His story is in Judges 11:29-40.

While many may question how he could have gone through with his vow, he and his daughter both understood what a terrible thing it was to go back on a vow that you had made to the Lord. Making a thoughtless vow to the Lord is certainly a sacrifice of fools, but breaking any vow to the Lord is also a sacrifice of fools with the consequence of God's wrath.

Have you ever been guilty of offering a sacrifice of fools? What does Solomon say? In Ecclesiastes 5:7, he states that many words are meaningless. This doesn't mean we aren't allowed to question God or to converse with Him. In fact, the very opposite is true. God wants us to be in a relationship with Him. However, we must revere and respect God and His position of authority and power.

Wrong Attitudes toward Possessions
Read Ecclesiastes 5:8-20. It can be hard not to combine the oppression of the poor with having a wrong attitude toward possessions. It seems that many people who do one do the other.

According to Solomon, describe the life of a rich person based on these verses.

_____

_____

_____

_____

Based on this, is having riches bad?

The balance is found in verses 18-19. It is good to enjoy the fruits of our labor and to enjoy the gifts that God has given. We must recognize that the ability to eat and drink and provide for our material needs is a gift from God. There is no other way to explain it and no other way to understand why we have the things we have. God has gifted them to us and we must treat them with respect.

If we understand that God has given us all these things as a gift, we will be able to follow the advice in verse 20. We must not dwell on the days of this life but be occupied with the joy that God gives us.

Conclusion

Think about all the fruits of your labor God has allowed you to enjoy. What is your attitude toward them? Have you thanked God for His provisions, or do you treat them like you are entitled to them? Do you hoard them, or are you prepared to give whatever to whomever whenever? Do you feel that they give you a sense of power? What would your life look like if you used all your "things" both to provide enjoyment for you as well as to bless others? Record your thoughts and any ideas you have on ways to live like everything you have is a gift from God.

Discussion Questions

1. Can you think of any other things people use as a means to power? How are those similar/different from the ones Solomon lists?

2. Is it possible to use these means to power for good? What would that look like?
3. When talking about the sacrifice of fools, how seriously do we take our words?
4. What is our attitude toward riches? How can it continue to move more in line with God's desire?

Session 6: Life

The things we get and the things we do. Most of us can sum up 99% of our lives as falling into one of those two categories. I work, so therefore I get paid money. I use the money to purchase things I think I need. I go out and do things around the house to improve my situation or my standing in society.

So why do we do these things and get these things? This can be a difficult question if you're looking for a deeper answer than, "I want them." Solomon, in his last final look around, lumps everything else into the category of "life."

Solomon's Observations: Life
Wealth
Read Ecclesiastes 6:1-2. What is the evil that Solomon has seen and is pointing out?

Having wealth is not evil. Read what the following verses have to say about wealth and summarize the main point of the verse.

Deuteronomy 8:17-18 _____

_____

Psalm 49:10 _____

_____

Psalm 112:3 _____

_____

Matthew 13:22 _____

_____

Luke 12:13-21 _____

_____

In some of these verses and situations, wealth is considered very good. In others, it is considered very bad. What makes the difference? The priority wealth has in our life. Seeking after wealth just to have wealth will not leave us satisfied or happy in life. Seeking after God and using whatever wealth He chooses to bless us with for His glory is the only way to find meaning in having the wealth in the first place.

Think about the ways you use money. Based solely on your use of money, not your thoughts or attitudes about money, what are high priorities in your life?

_____

_____

_____

Are you pleased with these as your priorities? Why or why not?

_____

_____

_____

Focus

Read Ecclesiastes 6:3-6. This passage contrasts two people. The first person lives a long life, has lots of children, but states that he is never satisfied. The second is one that has never been born, never sees the sun, and never knows anything of what this life has to offer. Why would Solomon say that the second person is the better of the two? This is a certainly a difficult and confusing concept to understand for those of us who are experiencing life right now.

If we look at this from a practical viewpoint, those of us who have lived on this earth and have seen the things that this world has to offer can be easily swayed to forget the greater good of our Heavenly Father. We can get caught up in the things of this world and not stay focused on Him. Solomon's point is that a person who has never been born is not tempted with this.

Actually, it is very easy to get caught up in the things of this world since we trust and believe our senses. This world with its real, tangible, touchable stuff competes greatly for our focus. Since we've never seen heaven or God with our own eyes, it can be very difficult to keep ourselves focused on the eternal. We must be diligent to maintain our focus on God.

For me, it is very easy to get caught up in all the things I'm doing during the day and forget about the eternal focus I should have. For that reason, I have set up what I call benchmarks in my life to help remind me. For example, I have pictures of people I'm praying for on my desk at work so that I am reminded to pray for them. I memorize Bible verses, and I review them at certain times of the day. I listen to Christian music in my car so that I can be hearing the praises of God even if I'm not in a praising mood at that moment. These benchmarks serve as reminders throughout the day that I need to keep my focus toward heaven and not get caught up in the things of this world.

Think about your day-to-day life. What benchmarks do you need to set up in order to bring your focus back on Christ throughout the day?

_____

_____

_____

Labor

Read Ecclesiastes 6:7-12. Solomon starts a review of all the things he has covered and observed. If I were to summarize the six verses, they'd go something like this.

Verse 7   Labor doesn't satisfy and all the things that we labor for do not satisfy

Verse 8	Having wisdom and acting wisely in this life doesn't satisfy
Verse 9	Enjoying what you have is better than dreaming about the things you don't, but in the end, neither satisfy
Verse 10	Creation has all been given its place in life and we cannot dispute that position
Verse 11	Being eloquent of speech of just speaking lots of words doesn't satisfy
Verse 12	Our lifetime here is limited and then it'll be over. It is all futile

Think back to your own quest to finding meaning in life. What are some areas you have observed other people trying? What have you found to give your life meaning?

_____

_____

_____

_____

Conclusion

Solomon is summing up all his observations. He's seen that time doesn't satisfy or give meaning to life. If anything, it keeps us unsettled and searching for more. He's seen that worldly justice is corrupt and there is no way to find meaning in that. He's seen power in both its good and bad uses, but it doesn't satisfy. He's observed people having improper attitudes about both God and their possessions that gave them no gain. And finally, he's looked over life in general and seen that there is no benefit to anything in life because it distracts us from who God is.

Now that Solomon has relayed all the things he has experimented with himself and all the things he's observed around him, he has some advice about living in this life to pass along, and we'll look at that next.

Discussion Questions
1. Have you ever wanted more money? Why?
2. How does having more money change our thoughts and focus on life?
3. What percentage of the day would you say you are focused on eternal things? What would your day look like if it was 50%? 75%?

Session 7: Describing Wisdom

Think back on all the pieces of advice you have received in your lifetime. From things as simple as "eat your vegetables" and "brush your teeth" to the more complex decisions regarding financial investments, choosing a spouse, or how to deal with a medical issue, we've all been given countless pieces of advice.

Advice is as common as a drop of water in the sea. How do we decide which pieces of advice we listen to and which ones we politely nod our head to and promptly forget? What filtering mechanism is in place to help us decide?

Several factors come into play, including the type of problem, our age, and our past experiences. But one of the main factors is whether or not we trust the person giving the advice. If we do not believe them to have our best interests in mind, or don't believe that they have a sufficient grasp of the problem, or if we do not feel they have the experience necessary, we tend to place less emphasis on that person's advice.

Solomon has just finished sharing his own experiences and his observations about life and finding the meaning of life. Now, he wants to offer some advice on how to live well in this life. We'll spend the next four sessions delving into Solomon's advice for us.

It is Better to Have Wisdom than Folly.

Solomon starts on familiar ground. His God-given wisdom has helped him through many situations during his reign as king. He has helped improve the land and added many levels of prosperity to the kingdom. Not surprisingly, he starts here and covers four main areas of using wisdom. We'll cover three in this session and one in the next.

Proverbs on Wisdom
Read Ecclesiastes 7:1-14.

Solomon is credited with writing most of the book of Proverbs, and he continues writing proverbs here. These proverbs deal with the subject of wisdom. Not surprisingly, several of them are echoed in the book of Proverbs as well. Remember, these are words of advice for how to succeed here in this life.

Reread these verses, and take a piece of paper and write down a keyword or phrase from each verse. If you'd like additional information, corresponding verses are listed in parentheses.

Verse 1 (Proverbs 22:1)_____

_____

Verse 2 (Psalm 90:12)_____

_____

Verse 3 (2 Corinthians 7:10)_____

_____

Verse 4 (Ecclesiastes 7:2)_____

_____

Verse 5 (Proverbs 6:23; 13:18; 15:31-21; 25:12)_____

_____

Verse 6 (Psalm 118:12)_____

_____

Verse 7 (Exodus 23:8; Deuteronomy 16:19)_____

_____

Verse 8 (Proverbs 14:29; Galatians 5:22-23)_____

_____

Verse 9 (James 1:19)_____

_____

Verse 10 (Matthew 6:34)_____

Verse 12 (Proverbs 8:35) _____

Verse 13 (Job 12:14; Isaiah 14:25) _____

Verse 14 (Job 2:10) _____

Solomon's proverbs cover a variety of areas where wisdom is used or abused. Verses 13 and 14 give us another glimpse into Solomon's ultimate conclusion. Only God has true wisdom concerning all things. He alone knows what is best and when it is best. Because of that, He is worthy of praise and glory in all things and at all times.

Wisdom and Life

Think about people you would consider righteous and those you would consider wicked. How do their lives compare? Are the righteous people always financially successful, or are the wicked people always punished for their wickedness? Do the righteous live long lives and the wicked die young? Solomon goes back to an overview about life. A person's righteousness or wickedness really has no effect on their length of life. However, Solomon will admit that wisdom does increase a person's chances for living longer. Read Ecclesiastes 7:15-18.

What do you think Solomon means when he states in verse 16, "Do not be excessively righteous and do not be overly wise"?

_____

_____

_____

_____

Compare this to the next verse where he states not to be excessively wicked or foolish. Another common theme throughout this book is the idea of balance and moderation. A person who is "excessively righteous or wise" can come across as arrogant or be tempted with pride. Neither of these would help that person succeed in life. We must be balanced and humble in our life. Ultimately, Solomon states that the fear of God is the most important thing above all of those other themes. Certainly, no one can be truly righteous or wise without recognizing this principle.

The Characteristics of Wisdom
I've been privileged to know some people I would consider truly wise in my life. Think about people you know who seem to have amazing wisdom. How would you describe them?

_____

_____

_____

_____

I am reminded of characteristics such as: calm but not passive, quiet but not overlooked, unassuming but never pushed around, thoughtful but not arrogant, soft-spoken yet every word they say holds enormous weight, patient but not lax in accountability, empathetic yet not condescending, satisfied with life.

Solomon is speaking about a few of these characteristics in Ecclesiastes 7:19-22. Read these verses.

Solomon recognizes that even the wisest of people do things that are wrong, but they know not to get caught up in the frivolous things of this world. So what if other people are saying negative things about you. Who cares if the rulers or people over you are not wise? You must seek to attain wisdom. You must seek to be wise, for true wisdom helps a person in this world far more than foolishness. A wise person will remember that, regardless of what happens on this earth, we are eternal beings and we will spend eternity in one of two places. Therefore, we should remain focused on the eternal things. Our relationship with God is the only thing that matters. Bringing Him glory and honor are the only things worth spending our time on (Matthew 6:33).

Solomon ends this chapter with another characteristic of wisdom: its rarity. Read Ecclesiastes 7:23-29.

We should all desire wisdom, yet what frequently happens (verses 23-24)?

_____

_____

So, if we can't attain true wisdom, why chase after it in the first place? The answer: we should seek God and Him only, and then we will be given the wisdom we need to deal with the issues that arise in this life.

What characteristics of wisdom do you see in your own life? What characteristics are lacking?

_____

_____

_____

_____

Conclusion

Since true wisdom only comes from God, if we are not seeking Him, we are doomed to a life more bitter than death and imprisoned by our own attempts to find pleasure and fulfillment. Unfortunately, like the verses in Matthew 7:13-14, only a few people actually find the right path to be on when it comes to seeking God.

> Enter through the narrow gate; for the gate is wide and the way is broad that leads to destruction, and there are many who enter through it. For the gate is small and the way is narrow that leads to life, and there are few who find it.

Next, we'll look at Solomon's advice on the uses of wisdom. Once a person is on the right path to seeking God and is given some degree of wisdom, it is important to know how to apply that wisdom.

Discussion Questions

1. What are some "wise" sayings you've heard? How do those compare with the wisdom Solomon gives in this chapter?
2. Have you experience times of being "overly wise?" How would you change those times?
3. How do you determine if someone is wise?

Session 8: Applying Wisdom to Life

As we discussed in the last session, we're looking at Solomon's advice to his listeners. He started with wisdom, a subject he is very familiar with. He gives us some basic proverbs on wisdom, discusses wisdom and life, and then lists some characteristics. Now, we're going to look at the application of wisdom. How should we use it?

It is Better to Have Wisdom than Folly.
Using Wisdom When Dealing with Those in Authority

I once had a friend who loved to boast about his ability to get out of speeding tickets. He would sit and explain all the intricacies of the legal system and the various loopholes he would exploit to get around the penalty for driving faster than the speed limit. I used to marvel at his seeming wisdom in dealing with those situations until I realized that he simply used it as an excuse for breaking the law. He would always drive over the speed limit everywhere he went, trusting in his abilities to get him off the hook later. After getting a couple of speeding tickets myself, I soon decided that his methods weren't exactly foolproof. Plus, the tickets consumed additional time, cost me money, and caused stress. I came to the same conclusion that Solomon did: for the most part, we should obey authority.

Read Ecclesiastes 8:1-9. What are the reasons Solomon gives for obeying authority (the king)?

_____

_____

_____

He lists several reasons, but an important one is in verse 2: "Keep the command of the king because of the oath before God." He is basically saying that God has placed that person in authority over you and you would be wise to keep their commands. This goes for any person in authority over you, including your boss, your parents, and all authority figures. Keeping their commands brings about a quiet, uneventful life that can be serene. Think about it. If you don't break the law, you're not constantly worried about the police chasing you, looking over your shoulder to see who's looking at what you're doing or worrying about getting caught. Wisdom would lead us to the conclusion that obedience is better than disobedience.

However, how do we handle it if the authority commands something that doesn't line up with God? Let me answer with an example.

I read a book by Brother Andrew entitled, "The Narrow Road." Brother Andrew is a Bible smuggler who, for decades now, has been taking God's Word into countries that are otherwise closed to the gospel. He works on the principle that if he can find any legal means of taking God's Word into a country, he uses it. However, if the authority of that country will not allow the legal transportation of the Bible into the country, then he will follow God's command to disciple and train others in Christ and will use an illegal means to transport Bibles. Now, each and every time he has used an illegal means, he has been fully prepared to experience that country's punishments if he should be caught. However, he recognizes that he is following God's authority, which is higher than man's.

Therefore, something needs to meet two criteria before we can be disobedient to human authority:

1) Does the command/law go against a specific command of God?
2) Are you prepared to experience the consequences from the earthly authority in the event you are found breaking the command/law?

Is your boss asking you to do something illegal or unethical? You need to follow God's commands of being upright and having integrity, but realize that you may lose your job. Given these criteria, the earlier example about the speeding tickets doesn't quite seem to hold up on either count, does it?

However, unless an authority has specifically asked you to do something contrary to God's commands, wisdom would instruct us to obey. As it says in verse 5, "He who keeps a royal command experiences no trouble." Besides, there are certain things that only God has authority over anyway, such as the wind or the day of death (verse 8). Wisdom leads us to obedience to authority—first God's authority, and then man's authority.

Using Wisdom with Wicked Men and with Righteous Men

Have you ever seen the movie Ocean's Eleven? In the remake of this movie starring George Clooney and Brad Pitt, the entire plot of the movie is centered around a bank heist. Danny Ocean and his group of ten other thieves plan an elaborate series of tricks and misdirection in order to steal over $160 million from three casinos owned by Terry Benedict. I find it interesting that while watching the movie, most people are actually rooting for the thieves to make off with the money. These are the same people who would say at another time that stealing is wrong and people shouldn't do it. Why then are we all so taken in by this plot of the movie? Simple. In the movie, Terry Benedict is made out to be a dishonest, sneaky, underhanded person who made his money through questionable means. A person's sense of justice takes over while watching. "Yes, he deserves to have all his money stolen because he's a bad guy."

In order for our sense of justice and fair play to be satisfied, we frequently find ourselves wishing for something bad to happen to "bad" people. Our logic is very basic; good things should happen to good people, and bad things should happen to bad people. The problem comes when the opposite happens.

Read Ecclesiastes 8:10-15. We're going to look at some of these verses more closely. Reread verses 11-13, and then read Psalm 50:16-21. Describe the thoughts and actions of an evil person.

_____

_____

_____

_____

God does not always punish an evil person immediately. Sometimes, an evil person prospers for years. Some people may look at that person and say that since he is doing well and "getting away with it" then they can do the same evil things. How does God reply to that mentality in Psalm 50:21?

_____

_____

_____

_____

Evil people will be judged for the bad things they have done. Solomon knew this. Even though it may seem to us like evil people are successful, God knows when their judgment will come. Solomon writes that we should fear God openly, in spite of whether others do or not. Solomon knew that sometimes it appears that bad things happen to good people and good things happen to bad people. However, God is over all, and in order to use wisdom when dealing with people, we must not try to imitate other people whether they are good or bad. We must openly fear God, strive to imitate Him, and leave everything else up to Him.

Using Wisdom When Dealing with God

Solomon sums up his discussions on the application of wisdom by looking at wisdom when used with God. He knows that God gave him wisdom for this life, so how does that compare to trying to know God?

Read Ecclesiastes 8:16-17. What is Solomon's conclusion regarding wisdom?

_____

_____

Bottom line: we can seek and search and try to use logic or reason to understand why things happen the way they do in life, but we'll never know or fully understand what God is doing or why He's doing it. This is the perfect contrast to earthly wisdom and Godly wisdom. Even though Solomon uses the same word wisdom, there really have been two different types of wisdom he's been discussing throughout this book. The first would be better understood as intelligence or smarts, and the second would be Godly wisdom that knows all things. God had given Solomon great intelligence and common sense to get through the difficulties and challenges that this world brings. However, Godly wisdom is not exactly the same thing. God is infinitely wise and understands the inner-workings of things far more than we ever could. People who have Godly wisdom understand that the answer to all questions is found in God and that sometimes He allows us to know the answers and sometimes He doesn't. When He does, we should rejoice and be ready and willing to share those answers with others. When He doesn't, we should still be ready and willing to trust Him and share our trust in Him with others.

Conclusion

In previous sessions, you described someone who you considered to be wise. Now that we've looked at two different types of wisdom, let's describe the characteristics of people with each type of wisdom. Remember, just because someone has one type of wisdom doesn't mean he or she has the other. List as many characteristics as you can think of.

Godly Wisdom_____

_____

_____

_____

_____

Earthly Intelligence_____

_____

_____

_____

_____

Where would you place yourself? Godly wisdom or earthly intelligence? Both? Neither? As we look back at the subject for the past two sessions, we realize that Solomon's point: "It is better to have wisdom than folly," refers primarily to earthly intelligence. True, if a person is given the choice, it is much easier getting through this life having intelligence as opposed to not having intelligence. However, only having intelligence is not enough because we are going to encounter things that do not make sense to us. Remember Ecclesiastes 3:10-15?

Godly wisdom provides more than intelligence; it provides trust and confidence in the Person who created everything and knows everything. Godly wisdom says, "I don't need to know everything; I just need to know the One who knows everything." This is the point Solomon has realized regarding the inadequacy of earthly intelligence, which he states in these last two verses. To paraphrase verses 16 and 17:

> I spent all my time and energy trying to understand and rationalize the things that are done here on earth, even to the point of losing sleep over them. I saw everything that God was doing or allowing to happen and I realized that I can never fully understand the things that are done here. Even if I sought constantly for my whole life, I'll never figure out why things are the way they are. If I ever meet someone who says they can rationalize things here on earth outside of God's wisdom, that person is either a liar or is deceived.

Solomon is starting to line out his conclusion, but he's still got some areas of advice that he needs to give first. Next session, we look at his advice about death.

Discussion Questions
1. Have you ever disagreed with authority? How did you handle that?
2. What are some situations where you would be following God's authority and going against man's authority?
3. How do you feel when God's doesn't immediately punish evil?
4. How can we better understand and be OK with God's timing in our lives?

Kristi Burchfiel

Session 9: Living to Die

I'm sure you've heard the saying, "Only two things in life are certain: death and taxes." My dad is a certified public accountant, and when it comes to the world of personal and corporate finances, this much I know: paying taxes is not a certainty. In fact, some people are really good at finding ways around paying their taxes. Others just simply don't pay their taxes and then wait to see what happens. On the contrary, if it is your time to die, there's really not going to be much you can do to get out of that.

We Will All Die Someday

Solomon understood that death is a certainty in this world. In fact, only one person had skipped death at the time Solomon wrote this, and that was Enoch, Adam's great-great-great-great grandson (Genesis 5). Now, that had been a long time ago, and several thousand (maybe million) other people had lived and died since that time, so death was considered a certainty to Solomon. In light of the fact that we are all going to die someday, Solomon wants us to examine our attitudes and actions in this life, recognizing that they have eternal consequences.

What Should Our Attitude Be?
Read Ecclesiastes 9:1-9. Solomon starts this chapter with his summary statement. Reread verses 1 and 2. What truth has Solomon taken to heart?

_____

_____

No matter what we do or don't do, whether we are righteous or wicked, obedient or disobedient, good or evil, we are all in the hands of God. God is in complete control of all things, and He holds them in His hands. Remember my statement from the very first session? "I can't trust myself to know or do what's best for me." Once I realized that was true, the next question automatically became, "Who can I trust?" The answer lies in these verses. All things are in the hands of God. We can trust God to hold us and to know more fully what we should be doing and not doing. Job reached the same conclusion after a long discussion with God. Read Job 42:1-6.

Once Job realized that he was not in control, what was his response? Repentance. He asked for forgiveness from God. Anytime we are confronted with the reality of the enormity and wisdom of God, we are forced to admit the insignificance of ourselves. Seeing God for who He really is is the best way to see ourselves. Because we are nothing and He is everything, He can mold us and make us into the person He wants us to be. We can trust Him to complete the work He has started in us (Philippians 1:6).

Once we have realized the truth from this verse, it doesn't mean that we should hide in a hole for the rest of our lives. Solomon goes on to explain that we, as the living, do have an advantage in one area over the dead. We have love, hate, and zeal while the dead do not (Ecclesiastes 9:6). We must have an attitude that we will love the things God loves, hate the things God hates, and be zealous for the things that God is zealous about. Having this attitude frees us to enjoy life the way God meant us to enjoy it, trusting in Him for everything that we have and everything that we need.

Think about your life. What areas do you like to control? What areas feel out of control? Take a few minutes and write a prayer to God, praising Him for being in control and repenting for any areas where you have tried to take control from Him.

_____

_____

_____

_____

_____

_____

What Should Our Actions Be?
Now that Solomon has explained the attitude that we should have, he goes into what our actions should be. Our attitude can have a profound effect on our actions. If we have the right attitude, our actions will fall in line. Read Ecclesiastes 9:10-12.

Other verses give the same idea. Summarize these verses.

Romans 12:11. _____

_____

Colossians 3:23. _____

_____

While we are living and have breath, we need to be doing the things that God has us here to do. How do we know what that is? God knows the plans He has for us and what He wants us to focus on, but like it says in verse 10, whatever we find to do, we should do it with all our might for His glory. What is that called? Integrity. This characteristic is one of four that one of my prior supervisors at work looked for in her employees. (The other three are honesty, teamwork, and professionalism.) You can't teach people integrity; they either have it or they don't. When she is interviewing people for positions, she tries to assess whether they are people with integrity. If we are following Christ, we will be people of integrity because we will be doing everything as if we were doing it for Him.

Even though we are all going to die someday, our actions now should reflect Christ. How do we apply this? Solomon gives us an example. Read Ecclesiastes 9:13-15.

Solomon tells a story. A city is under siege from a strong and mighty army. With the prospect of imminent destruction, one wise man steps forward and decides to do what he can to intercede for the people of the city. He seeks an audience with the commander of the army, they reach an agreement, and the city is spared. This wise peacemaker then fades into history, and he and his deed of heroism is forgotten. Whether Solomon is making this story up or remembering a story he heard from his father David (See 2 Samuel 20:14-22) really doesn't matter; the conclusion is the same. Our actions should be the same regardless of whether they will give us great fame or not. Since Solomon has already established that we will all die someday, this person didn't act out of fear of death but rather out of a desire for peace.

Have you ever been a peacemaker between two people who were at odds with one another? Describe your experience. Were the two people reconciled? Were they grateful for your involvement?

_____

_____

_____

_____

Regardless of the outcome between the two people, acting like Christ means we make ourselves available to do the things He would do. This may mean that we are not appreciated or remembered. Or we may be greatly appreciated and exalted. Either way, this does not change how we conduct ourselves or the actions we take.

Solomon has used this chapter to give us advice on how to live in light of the fact that we will die. Read the last three verses of the chapter, Ecclesiastes 9:16-18.

Having wisdom is indeed better in all circumstances in this life. It helps us to respond to situations correctly and wisdom reminds us that even if we are not publicly acknowledged for our actions, that's okay. We are to have the same attitude as Christ and act in the same manner as Christ.

As one final thought, read Philippians 2:5-8. Describe what it means to have the same attitude as Christ.

_____

_____

_____

Describe Christ's actions since He had that attitude.

_____

_____

_____

How can you demonstrate the attitude and actions of Christ in your life?

_____

_____

_____

Conclusion

We are all going to die someday. Because of that, Solomon advises us to be conscious of how we live while we are still alive. Are we having the attitude of Christ? Are we acting as Christ would act? Solomon is going to give us his last piece of advice in the next session, and it comes back to the closing statements of this chapter: wisdom verses foolishness.

Discussion Questions
1. Have you thought about your death before? What actions or steps have you taken to prepare for that?
2. If you knew you had 24 hours to live, what would you do differently? Would that change if it was 6 months instead?
3. Christ came to earth knowing exactly how long He would live and when He would die. Looking back at His life, how did that knowledge shape the way He lived each day?

Kristi Burchfiel

Session 10: The Fool and His Reward

"What could possibly go wrong?" This question has been asked in countless books and movies, usually right before everything imaginable (and sometimes unimaginable) happens to go wrong. Being able to determine the possible consequences of our actions before acting is a definite sign of intelligence, and it also goes a long way in helping us to avoid some of the common pitfalls of life.

I've been told many stories by people who are wondering how they ended up with their lives in such a mess. Frequently, they can trace things back to a particular decision they made to do something they shouldn't have. From there, they followed a string of poor decisions that led them to where they are now. Generally, they never thought one poor decision could start them on a path to such lows. We are all one poor decision away from such a path. So, how do we avoid the path of the fool?

Foolishness is Detrimental to All

Solomon, in his wisdom, actually wrote a lot about the difference between wisdom and foolishness (or folly). The book of Proverbs includes numerous admonitions to be careful, watch out, and to avoid folly in all its forms. Solomon had also written earlier in Ecclesiastes about the advantages of having wisdom while here in this life. He also had come to the realization that being wise on this earth is not the end-all and be-all of our existence. I think it is interesting that Solomon puts this chapter after one about death. Solomon has gotten his understanding in line. Death is going to happen to us all and we should have the right attitude and do the right actions in the meantime as discussed in the previous session. However, while we're here, it is definitely better to be wise than to be a fool because our actions here have eternal consequences.

Foolishness and Wisdom: The Contrast

Solomon starts out with a contrast of wisdom and foolishness. Read Ecclesiastes 10:1-7.

The summary: a little foolishness goes a long way. The group Casting Crowns has a song out entitled "Slow Fade." The idea is very simple; many of the big messes we find ourselves in didn't become big overnight. Oftentimes, they start out as small decisions to compromise our beliefs. These then lead us steadily downhill until we become completely overwhelmed. This is the same idea Solomon is sharing from verse one.

Verse 3 is also especially important. Reread verse 3. Have you ever known a person who was acting like a fool but refused to believe it when others pointed out the foolishness of his/her actions?

I've had a couple of different family members who have made poor choices and started down the path of fools. Unfortunately, when they were lovingly confronted with the consequences of their decisions by members of the family, they refused to believe they had made poor choices. These people kept right on doing what they had been doing, to the extreme detriment of themselves and their loved ones.

There are a couple of ways to respond when dealing with a foolish person. A perfect illustration of both is found in 1 Samuel 25:2-35. Take a few minutes and read the story of Nabal, a fool, and David and Abigail.

In this story, Nabal refuses to give David and his soldiers any food or bread even though David's soldiers had treated him kindly.

How does David respond?_____

_____

What would have been the result?_____

_____

Before David's plan is put into action, Abigail finds out about her husband Nabal's refusal. She also responds.

How does Abigail respond?_____

_____

What was the result?_____

_____

Maintaining calmness and Godly wisdom is the only way to deal with fools. Abigail knew that her husband was in the wrong, and she took steps to ensure his protection as well as the protection for her entire household. Just as Solomon states, it is much better to live with wisdom than foolishness.

Foolishness and Wisdom: The Actions

Our actions are very telling to others when it comes to whether we are operating under foolishness or intelligence. Being able to use common sense is a very important trait, and Solomon lists some examples in the next few verses.

Read Ecclesiastes 10:8-15. List all the daily actions that are mentioned here.

_____

_____

_____

_____

_____

Digging a pit, demolishing a wall, dealing with animals, speaking, and working all made the list. In each of these, it is shown how a person can be foolish while doing these things.

This section reminds me of those animal television shows that always have some professional person traveling to some dark, deep jungle to spend time pulling snakes out of holes so they can be measured or tagged or something. The camera follows him as he steps up to a hole and sticks his arm in, warning us to not try this at home. I'm always thinking, *Why try it at all?* Still, we all have daily responsibilities that need to get done, but we need to use common sense when doing them. Safety is important, and failure to utilize the appropriate safety procedures can result in great injury. Only a fool would sacrifice safety regardless of the perceived benefit.

One particular area we're going to discuss in more detail is in verses 12-13: words. These can so easily be used foolishly. Mark Twain once said, "It is better to keep your mouth closed and let people think you are a fool than to open it and remove all doubt." Unfortunately, we don't always heed this piece of advice.

Read James 3:2-10. James tries to describe the power that the tongue has. How would you describe the power and influence of the tongue?

_____

_____

_____

The wrong word at the wrong time spoken in the wrong way can have a long-lasting, negative effect. At the same time, the right word spoken at the right time in the right way can do a profound amount of good. What makes the difference? The answer is found in 1 Corinthians 13:1.

_____

_____

If love, genuine love, as defined in 1 Corinthians 13:4-9, is the motivation through which we are speaking or doing any of the daily actions listed in this passage in Ecclesiastes, then we are going to be able to achieve the actions of wisdom.

Foolishness and Wisdom: The Effect on Others

As mentioned before, a person acting foolishly doesn't do it in a vacuum. Frequently, their actions also have a negative impact on those around them. Solomon ends this chapter by discussing this point.

Read Ecclesiastes 10:16-20. As the ruler of the land is, so is the country. A foolish leader is a detriment to his country, and a wise leader is an asset.

Two ideas come to mind when I read verse 20. The first: if you can't say something nice, don't say anything at all. This has been stated by mothers, fathers, grandmothers, Sunday school teachers, and counselors everywhere. This is a good piece of advice, as it will keep you out of a whole bunch of problems.

The second is more indirect. I remember coming home from having done something I shouldn't have just to find out that my mother already knew about it. How did she know? I would ask. The answer: "A little birdie told me." Apparently, this bird has been around for a very long time, as he was sharing information and secrets back in Solomon's day. Somehow, even the most secret of secrets gets found out and told. If we truly want to avoid regrets, we must realize that we are to be very careful what we say about others or situations because you never know who is listening. This is especially true in today's society of instant and widespread information. Who knows? Someone might catch you saying something you'd regret in a video on his or her cell phone and then post it on the Internet.

Conclusion

Bottom line: when striving to live a life without regrets, we must take an inventory of our actions and determine whether they are foolish or not. Frequently, it is a slow descent into the realm of compromise that leads us to depths we never thought we were capable of going to. How do we avoid this? Seek wisdom from God, examine ourselves for areas we have compromised, open ourselves up to a trustworthy and godly friend who will hold us accountable.

As we close this section of advice from Solomon, we must realize that wisdom has played a key theme in his advice. We must understand wisdom, seek wisdom in this life, know the benefits of wisdom, and actually use the wisdom we have. We must recognize that we are all going to die someday, so our attitude and actions should reflect that our focus is on eternal things. Also, we must understand what it means to be a fool and how to guard against acting like a fool. Next session begins the detailing of Solomon's conclusions from all his experiments, observations, and advice.

Spend the last few moments of this session in prayer to God. Ask him to show you any areas where you may have compromised His principles and thus started a slow descent to foolishness. Ask forgiveness for any issues where your actions may have been hurtful or detrimental to others. He stands ready to forgive and to restore (1 John 1:9). Ask Him to provide you with someone to help you stay accountable so you don't slip back into your habits. Record any thoughts or prayers God leads you to make.

_____

_____

Discussion Questions
1. Do you consider yourself wise or foolish? Why?
2. Some people seem to act wisely in one area of their lives, but then very foolishly in another area. Why do you think that happens?
3. How have you been impacted by the foolishness of others? How has your foolishness impacted others? How does forgiveness address both situations?

Session 11: Attitude Adjustment

"You need an attitude adjustment." I heard those words frequently throughout my adolescent life. I would be upset about something or not getting my way in some area, and I would display my displeasure for everyone to see. From what I can tell, that's a fairly common occurrence in today's world. A person's attitude toward their circumstances shapes literally everything from their thoughts on a subject to the way they present themselves to other people to even their physical health. Several branches of psychology devote a large portion of their energy to studying both how the attitude affects life as well as how a person can modify his attitude to improve his life.

> Life is 10 percent what you make it, and 90 percent how you take it.
>
> Irving Berlin

Solomon has been through ten chapters explaining his perception of life, sharing his experiments, detailing his observations, and recounting his advice. We've looked at the futility of material possessions, the pointlessness of long life, the gains of evil people, and the consequences of foolishness. Throughout the book, Solomon has continued stating that everything is meaningless or vanity. Now Solomon is ready to move from telling us what not to do toward telling us what to do in order to live a life without regrets. He starts by having us analyze our attitude in four specific areas: others, the future, work, and life.

Attitude toward Others

As much as I would like to say that I get along with everyone, unfortunately that just isn't the case. There can be many reasons for this, but sometimes there just seems to be some difference of opinion that gets in the way of communication. Many of you can relate to this. Occasionally, this situation comes up with people that we are required to work with in some form or fashion. How do we deal with people we'd rather not deal with?

Read Ecclesiastes 11:1-2.

These verses deal with a very specific attitude that comes up frequently around other people: egocentrism, or the "it's all about me" attitude. This attitude can be counteracted by two important principles: risktaking and generosity. Let me define these concepts as they deal with relationships.

1) Risktaking—Be willing to see and act on the positive in people regardless of whether they deserve it or have earned it.
2) Generosity—Freely offer everything you have to others, including money, time, advice, or resources, among other things.

Frequently, these two attitudes overlap. However, there are subtle differences. Taking a risk on people means putting yourself in a position to help someone who doesn't deserve it, even if it requires sacrifice on our part. It also means we open ourselves up to the possibility of being hurt. Generosity refers to the giving of something and not holding them accountable to pay you back. Read the following verses, and summarize what they say about risktaking and generosity.

Proverbs 19:17. _____

_____

_____

Matthew 10:42. _____

_____

_____

Matthew 5:42. _____

_____

_____

Galatians 6:9. _____

_____

_____

1 Timothy 6:18-19. _____

_____

_____

Romans 12:17-21. _____

_____

_____

In order for us to avoid having regrets, we must adjust our attitude about people so that it lines up with how God views people, which includes taking risks on people and being generous toward them.

Take a few minutes and think about the person (or people) that you clash with. How does God see that person? What positive characteristics did He give them that you hadn't noticed before? Take a few minutes, and pray that God will help you see them the way He sees them.

Attitude toward the Future

Many dollars are poured away year after year by people seeking to know and understand the future. Psychics have hotlines for people to call, shops where people can have their palms read, and almost every major newspaper in the country lists a person's daily horoscope. Solomon discussed earlier our burning desire to know and understand the future. However, here, he briefly touches on it again.

Read Ecclesiastes 11:3-5.
Some people are so consumed by their "need" to know the future that it prevents them from doing anything now. Solomon is reminding us that just because we do not understand how God works doesn't mean we shouldn't act or respond. We don't always have to know the "how" in order to be effective. Plus, if we're always waiting to act until we understand everything, that doesn't leave much room for faith.

Consider the story of Nicodemus found in John 3:1-21.

Nicodemus was an important teacher and ruler during the time of Jesus. He knew almost everything that could be known about the Jewish law and the ins and outs of practicing a devout, godly life. However, when he heard about Jesus, he was perplexed. He went and met with Jesus secretly. Jesus made a profound statement: "Unless one is born again, he cannot see the kingdom of God." This highly educated man went about trying to make sense of this statement, so he asked Jesus, "How can this be?" Jesus then spends the rest of the discussion explaining that God can do things that defy our comprehension and that we do not need to understand the intricate details of how He does them; we just need to know that He can do them.

How is it that God in His infinite wisdom and power can move in such a way that a mere human who is nothing more than a breath can be able to experience the saving grace and mercy of God? No one on earth will ever be able to explain exactly what the Holy Spirit does in us that allows us to come into a personal relationship with Jesus Christ. Thankfully we don't have to understand it for it to be true. We are invited by Christ to come and lay our sins down and experience true, saving forgiveness; be made truly clean in His sight; and reign with Him in heaven one day. I know that is true, but the exact process is a mystery.

The same is true with the future. Our attitude needs to be one of trusting God and leaning on Him for guidance and not trying to spend our time searching through for the exact logic to plan the future. Until we can have faith in Him to take care of the future for us, we'll never have the right attitude.

What concerns are you facing? What areas create anxiety and worry for you? As you think about what tomorrow might bring, are you scared? Spend a few moments in prayer to God, asking Him to help you let go of an attitude of control over the future.

Attitude toward Work

The word work can be very misleading. Most people think it refers to a person's employment or career. However, Solomon is using a much broader idea of work in this passage. He refers to anything that you do or any responsibilities you have.

Read Ecclesiastes 11:6-7.

Like many examples in the Bible, Solomon uses a farming example. When should a person sow seed in order to have an abundant harvest? His answer: all the time. Having the right attitude toward the responsibilities we have in our lives means that we are always ready for those responsibilities and are never caught off guard. Another important verse regarding our attitude toward our responsibilities is found in 1 Corinthians 10:31. If you read the verses before and after it, the verse actually admonishes us to do what we are doing for the glory of God, regardless of who is watching. This is another reference to integrity and consistency in our walk.

Think about your normal day. How do you get up in the morning? How do you treat your family while everyone is getting ready to head out for the day? How do you spend your free time? What do you look at on the Internet? What jokes do you laugh at or repeat to others?

Now, would any of those activities change if someone followed you around all day? Would you censor your jokes, avoid some of your co-workers for fear of what they might say about you or to you? Would you spend your free time differently?

Ecclesiastes 11:6 deals with this issue of laziness and making sure that you are doing all that you should be doing. Verse 7 refers to doing things in an open, upstanding way or in "the light."

Which issue do you struggle with more, laziness or openness?

Sowing seeds is also used frequently in the Bible as an analogy for witnessing. The same applies here. You never know when your witness to someone will be exactly what he or she needs to see or hear. Besides, as followers of Christ, we do actually have Christ with us at all times, whether we want to acknowledge that or not.

Pretend you are an outsider looking at your life. Would you be pointed to Christ by the actions and attitudes you observed?

Write down two areas of responsibility that you need to address so that you can have the right attitude toward your work. How do they need to be addressed? What specific plans or actions do you need to take in order to have a work life focused on Christ?

_____

_____

_____

_____

Attitude toward Life

Solomon follows this up with a look at our life. This refers to the importance that God places on our lives; after all, He gave it to us (Genesis 1:27), and He knows everything about us (Psalm 139).

Read Ecclesiastes 11:8-10. What is your first reaction to how Solomon states we should spend our lives, especially in verse 9?

_____

_____

_____

Many people have used these verses to justify doing whatever they wanted to with their lives. I've heard people talk about how important it is to do whatever pleases you and looks good. After all, verse 9 does say that a young man should "follow the impulses of your heart and the desire of your eyes." How does this idea of doing whatever feels good compare or contrast with what you've been taught or heard about Christianity?

_____

_____

_____

There's a large spectrum of thinking on this idea, so let me give you the two extremes.

First, the idea many people have grown up with is that God is a stern judge sitting in heaven with His list of rules waiting for us to mess up so He can zap us. Somehow, that has never been a big selling point in trying to persuade people to give their lives to Christ. Personally, my favorite phrase to sum up this attitude is the "Cosmic Killjoy." Doesn't that evoke an image of terror and fright? I mean, with a God like that, you'd better mind your p's and q's and not put one toe out of line, or you'll face the consequences.

Second, in response to that idea, there's the thought that God loves everyone and doesn't care what you do or how you do it. If it feels good, then God meant for you to do it. We should be free to accept anything, tolerate everything, and if we want something, there's no reason to deny ourselves. This idea has been around in various fashions over the last several centuries and currently has turned into the concept of tolerance and acceptance of whatever that permeates our culture today.

If you subscribe to either of these ideas, then verse 9 is going to create problems for you. On the one hand, a person who subscribes to the first idea would be appalled at Solomon's statement that we should follow the impulses of our heart. However, a person subscribing to the second idea would not have an answer to the next sentence in verse 9: "Yet know that God will bring you into judgment for all these things."

The answer, as so often happens, lies in the middle of this spectrum. God wants us to have fun and enjoy our lives. However, God also knows what things are in our best interest and will actually cause us harm later on. Some things we think might be fun now actually cause heartache and distress later. God wants us to avoid those things. On the second hand, we are going to answer to Him someday for our actions and decisions, and so those should be made based on His desires for our life.

The verse that best illustrates this middle ground is John 14:15. Jesus is speaking, and He states, "If you love Me, you will keep My commandments." Love is the key. Having a relationship with Christ involves loving Him and being loved by Him. If we truly love Him, we will want to do everything He has said, requested, commanded, or asked us to do. Why? Not because a bolt of lightning might come down from heaven and roast us, but because we love Him and want to please Him. This is the attitude we should have toward life.

God wants us to enjoy ourselves, get together and laugh and have fun, and to take pleasure in the things that He has created in this world. However, He understands that to have the most enjoyment in those things, we must use them as He intended and follow His instructions.

By the same token, God does not tolerate everything here on earth because it goes against His will and what He has established as being the best for us. Because of this, there will be judgment of the things of this world that are sin. He is Holy and He cannot be in the presence of sin.

How do we practice this? The more we get to know God, the more we understand His love for us, and we love Him in return. The more we love Him the more we keep His commandments. The more we keep His commandments the easier it is to find joy in those things that are pleasing to God. The more we find joy in the things of God the more we want to know Him.

Love God, and keep His commandments. This is the attitude we should have toward life in general, for only then can we truly enjoy the things this world has to offer.

Conclusion

As we listen to Solomon's conclusions, we are told to have an attitude adjustment. We need to examine our attitudes toward others, the future, work, and life. Where are you at? What adjustments need to be made? Think about which of these four areas are the furthest out of alignment. What are some ways to start making the adjustments needed?

Solomon is nearing the end. With only one session to go, we are going to spend it examining Solomon's final conclusion and how to apply it to our lives.

Discussion Questions
1. Give an example of a time you've taken a risk on someone? What about a time you've been generous?
2. How much do you desire to know the future? What are you inadvertently sacrificing now while you are focused on what's to come?

3. How do you view God? How do you reconcile the truth that God is love with the truth that God is holy?

Session 12: Enhance Your Memory

The movie Fifty First Dates, starring Adam Sandler and Drew Barrymore, tells the story of a man who falls in love with a woman, only to realize that she had previously been in an accident and suffered a brain injury. This injury kept her from remembering anything that had happened to her since that accident, and she essentially relived the same day over and over again. Adam Sandler worked every day to introduce himself to her and get her to fall in love with him before she fell asleep and he had to start all over again the next day. It's a comedic answer to the question, "What if we had no memory?"

Our memories are very important to us. Without them, we cannot remember our phone number, our family, our purpose for driving to the grocery store—anything. We wouldn't know where we're going and would have no idea where we've been. Memory is the last area Solomon covers, and it is where he finalizes his conclusions. Four areas should be burned into our memories.

Remember Your Past

Read Ecclesiastes 12:1-4. Write down the thoughts, feelings, or impressions you have when you think back to your childhood.

_____

_____

_____

_____

Some people will have very positive, happy thoughts about family time, siblings, playing outdoors, and being carefree. Others will not have such positive, happy memories, and their ideas will include sadness, anger, abuse, or neglect. Most of us fall somewhere in the middle. My childhood was a mixture of climbing trees and running through fields with difficult peer relationships and the feelings of awkwardness. Why does Solomon want us to remember these things?

Well, children typically have fewer worries than adults. They're supposed to know less of the struggles and responsibilities that adults experience. Children also have an easier time with the concept of faith. Children are generally trusting and accept ideas exactly as they are explained. This is also why children must be protected. Read Matthew 18:1-6.

So then why is it important to remember your past? We must remember what it was like to be a child, trusting and innocent. As Solomon puts it, "before the evil days come," we are able to remember the Creator. We come to God like a child (Mark 10:15). We must remember our past before we were caught up in the responsibilities and trappings of this world.

Think about what draws you away from God. What worries draw your attention away from what God has done? What fears overtake your mind? What regrets keep you chained? What burdens weigh you down? What would it be like if you were able to hand those over to God once and for all? Read Micah 7:18-19. God wants us to be free from these fears, burdens, and regrets. He wants us to give them to Him and not take them back. Spend a few minutes describing your life as God wants to make it: free from the worries, fears, burdens, and regrets.

_____

_____

_____

_____

_____

_____

_____

When we place our faith in Christ, God takes all those worries and burdens, and he removes them. We do not have to fear Him anymore, only run to Him. That first moment when we experience new life in Christ is when our true sense of self is confirmed. This is the moment when our faith and trust is completely in Christ. We don't know how He's going to do it all, and we don't know what He's going to ask of us, but we don't care. It's enough just to bask in the peace and rest of our Father and know that He loves us. This is your true past as God sees it. Remember it.

Remember Your Future

From looking backward to looking forward, Solomon shifts his focus to the things to come. Read Ecclesiastes 12:5-8.

This is certainly not the first time Solomon has spoken about the inevitability of death. This life is going to end for all of us someday. Solomon has already told us to have the right attitude toward this life since we are going to die. What is the danger of forgetting the future? Read Matthew 6:19-21.

_____

_____

_____

The question that begs to be asked is: Where is your treasure? Are you seeking to lay up earthly treasures and the wealth of this world, or are you desperately seeking treasure in heaven and searching for that which makes one "heavenly" rich?

Recently, God has convicted me of hoarding stuff—not money specifically, but stuff. You know, the things that lie around our house in back closets or attics just waiting for that one specific moment in time when, "I'm sure I'll need it." So I told God, "Okay. I'll sell it, so that way I can use the money." I unloaded my things and laid them out, took pictures of them, and went to work trying to sell them on eBay. Would you believe not one thing sold? Nothing. I finally realized that selling was my way of fixing the problem, but it wasn't teaching me to stop laying up treasure in this world. I was just exchanging my treasure from stuff to money. I realized I needed to give my stuff away, and it needed to be to someone or some organization that couldn't pay me back—no tax deductions, no credit, nothing. I needed to be willing to just let it go. Why? God used this to teach me that I need to trust Him to provide for everything. Hoarding things is just the same as hoarding money, and neither gives treasure in heaven. Does this mean you need to do the same thing? Not necessarily. I just know it was the right thing for me to do. You may have a different way of storing up treasure in this world that God wants to address with you.

So, what are you hoarding? Where are you laying up treasure? Nothing here is going to last—only those things we lay up in heaven. Spend some time recording any thoughts God has given you about what you are hoarding here on earth and what you should do about it.

_____

_____

_____

_____

Where is your treasure? Remember your future, and plan your treasure accordingly.

Remember Truth

Truth has become increasingly subjective these days. Standing on something as the "truth" can be most unpopular, especially if it disagrees with what other people perceive as truth. The question becomes: What is truth?

Before we move to define truth, we must also note that the writing of Ecclesiastes has changed. No longer are we listening to his sermon. Like many books, this one includes a biography of the author at the very end. Read Ecclesiastes 12:9-12. What are Solomon's accomplishments as they are listed here?

_____

_____

_____

He was wise. He wrote proverbs. He taught people, and he sought to write words of truth correctly. "Words of truth," is a very important phrase. Truth is what is used to move people along down the path of life. Truth is like a well-driven nail that holds things together exactly as they should be. Solomon even tells us where words of truth come from in verse 11. Truth is given by one Shepherd. This is reference to God and is also a word used to describe Jesus Christ. Many of these very words are used to describe Jesus.

Read John 1:1, 14; John 10:11; John 14:6. How is Jesus described?

_____

_____

_____

Looking back at the list you just created, compare that to the verses in Ecclesiastes. Circle all the words above that are found in Ecclesiastes 12:9-12.

Can there be any doubt where truth really comes from? Anything apart from Jesus is not really truth. He's more than just simply telling us truth, Jesus is truth. The two cannot be separated. The truth in every area of life begins and ends with Jesus. This concept can be difficult to understand completely. But like God's ability to save us, which was discussed earlier, this does not have to be completely understood, just accepted based on the descriptions of Jesus we listed from the Bible.

What areas in your life have you compromised? Which ones aren't guided solely by the Truth? In what area have you been accepting of things that really aren't truth at all? Record those areas here, and then spend a few minutes in prayer that God will help you get them back in line with His Truth.

_____

_____

_____

_____

In order to remember truth, we must know Christ. Truth is loving, kind, compassionate, yet steadfast and certain. Truth meets people where they are but isn't content to leave them there. Get to know Christ and allow Him to rule your life, for that is the only way to live out Truth. Remember Christ. Remember Truth.

Remember God

I am a "bottom line" person. I'm good at reading through material or listening to material and summarizing it into a couple of sentences. Solomon concludes the book by giving us a bottom line.

Read Ecclesiastes 12:13-14. What is Solomon's bottom line?

_____

_____

Fear God, and keep His commandments. Why should we do that? It applies to every person, and, ultimately, we're going to answer to God for all we have done anyway.

This word fear frequently gets misconstrued. This doesn't refer to the "hide in a corner" type of fear. This word is used to represent respect and awe. We need to have respect and awe for the position that God has over us. In fact, since I'm going to answer to Him for my deeds someday, this is something I'd want to remember on a regular basis so that it would guide what I do and how I do it. Ultimately, our response to God's gift of His Son, Jesus Christ will determine the initial outcome of that judgment, but realize that, even after that, we are going to have to answer for our deeds.

Read John 14:21. Why do we obey God's commandments?

_____

Many times, we get this backward. We believe that we must do things for God. In actuality, we are to love God, and because we love Him, we obey Him. If we do not truly love God, we find the obedience part to be nothing more than a listing of rules. If we love Him, they become opportunities to show Him we love Him. The perspective is totally different.

When was the last time you thought about loving God—not doing something for Him, not getting something from Him, just loving Him? He deserves to be loved, and He loves us tremendously. Many passages in the Bible talk about loving God, but one of the best is Psalm 119. The entire chapter is a love song devoted to God's Word. Since God's Word is Jesus, based on John 1:1, 14, it is literally a love chapter to God. Make time in the next few days to read through the entire chapter and focus on loving God. For now, read through Psalm 119: 129-136.

Write a prayer to God based on what you learn about God through these verses.

_____

_____

_____

_____

_____

_____

The bottom line: remember God, and everything else will fall into place.

Conclusion

Memory was very important to the people of Israel in the Old Testament. In Hebrew, the word for memory used is *zakar*. Interestingly, when God did something amazing for the people, he would instruct them to build a *zikkaron* or a memorial so they would have a visual reminder of the work that God had done in their life or for their people (Joshua 4:1-7, for example). This way, people would have no excuse for not remembering God's faithfulness and protection to them in the past. That memorial would serve as a reminder of past care and protection from God and help them trust that He would care for them in the future.

Many things can serve as reminders for us today. We can use physical or tangible items, or we can simply tell the story to others, describing what God has done for us. Remembering each of these four areas is the key to living a life without regrets. Take a few minutes, and write down your responses to each of these four areas as a memorial you can return to when you need reminding of what God has for you.

My Memorial
Remember Your Past.
What has God done or provided for you in the past? What is it like when you remember only that He loves you and you love Him?

_____

_____

_____

_____

_____

_____

Remember Your Future.
What have you decided to stop hoarding here on earth? What heavenly treasures are you pursuing?

_____

_____

_____

_____

_____

_____

Remember Truth.
What areas of your life do you refuse to compromise anymore? How are you going to get to know the truth in Jesus better?

_____

_____

_____

_____

_____

Remember God.
In what ways are you going to demonstrate your love for God more?

_____

_____

_____

_____

_____

How do we live a life without regrets? Remember these four areas specifically and tailor your actions around them. Thinking back to the very beginning of this study, only Jesus is ever going to have a completely regret-free life. But if we have accepted Jesus as our personal Savior and are allowing Him to have control and guide us, He will always lead us the appropriate way.

Do you have past regrets? Give them to Him. Seek His forgiveness and His love.

Do you want to live without regrets? Learn from the example set for us by Solomon in Ecclesiastes. At the end of his life, he realized that only by letting go of his plans and fearing God is it possible to find any kind of meaning in this life. Remember God.

Discussion Questions
1. How has your past influenced your present? How do you intend to allow it to influence your future?
2. How have you overlooked truth in your life? How would your life be changed if you truly believe that Jesus is truth?
3. Looking at your life, how would placing God first in your life help you live Without Regrets?

Leader's Guide

As I put together this second edition, I wanted to provide some additional resources for those who choose to participate in this study as a group. For those of you who have volunteered to lead a group study of *Without Regrets,* congratulations! Learning in a group is always a great way to really expound on the principles that are found in a study. Leading the study gives you an opportunity to be used by God to help shape that learning for others. God always has a great way of using the insights of others to continue to help us to learn more.

This Leader's Guide is split into two main sections. First, I will provide some overall tips for how to set up a group and what to expect as the leader of a group. If this is your first time leading a Bible Study group, you may find these particularly helpful. If you've led several groups in the past, hopefully you'll find a few things in there as well that you haven't thought about. These principles apply to most every

Bible Study group I've ever led or been a part of and it's always good to review.

Second, I will give some key thoughts or focuses to bring out for each session. The Discussion Questions at the end of each session are another great resource to help spark discussion in the group. Here, these will focus on key takeaways and application to help the discussion remain focused on the topic for that session.

As always, the Holy Spirit is the guide to help us understand and apply the scripture. As you lead the group, He is the One who prompts us and leads us as we learn and grow together. Prayerfully seek His guidance throughout the entire study.

Leading a Small Group

When you agree to leading a small group, especially if it is your first time to do so, there is a certain amount of nervousness and fear that most people feel. First, take a minute to congratulate yourself on being brave enough to step out by faith to do this in the first place. As you start thinking about the group, there are some set up and logistical types of questions that may come up. I'll list out several things to just think about. Realize these are not meant to feel overwhelming and there's no right or wrong answer to these. Some of the best groups are set up the simplest. I am just a fan of planning!

Set Up
1. Where and when are you going to have the group? A consistent meeting time and place goes a long way in ensuring the success of the group.
2. Do people know how to get there and are there any challenges? If you're holding this at a main location, such as a church, this may not be much of an issue,

but if it's in a home, apartment numbers, parking options, building codes, and other things are all important to consider and to ensure that everyone attending knows.
3. Food or no food? Some people like to study while they share a meal. Others enjoy snacks. Some have no food at all. The timing and location of the group have a lot to do with the answer to this one, but it's something to think about.
4. Childcare. This may or may not be an issue, depending on who is in the group, but it's always a good question to ask and to work with other leaders to determine what options are available, if needed.
5. Group set up. Once you've picked the location, take a quick look around to review what the group may prefer for a set up. Table and chairs? Couches? In a circle? Scattered throughout the room? Take into consideration the group preferences, but also keep in mind what setting helps everyone stay focused on the group and each other.
6. Participants. You may or may not have a choice in participants, but wherever possible, I like to include as much diversity as possible in a group. Diversity would include age, ethnicity, background, life experiences, personality types, etc. I find that the discussions become more insightful when people share from their own unique perspective.

During the Meetings
1. Start and end with prayer. This sounds like it would be easy to do, but I have found that it's important to be intentional with this because it's easy to get caught up "leading" the meeting and forget. Make sure and take the time to meet with Jesus. Without Him, there's really no point.

2. Invite and encourage participation from the group. Some groups take a couple of weeks to warm up to each other, but be sure they know that you want to hear from them.
3. Don't be the only one talking. As the leader, your goal is to "lead" the group discussion, not dominate it. This is not about just your ideas and thoughts. If you're talking more than 50% of the time, you're talking too much.
4. Stay in control of the discussion topics. If you have a few talkative folks in the group, this can be a challenge. Your goal as the leader is to keep the discussion centered on the topics at hand. If you find the conversation veering off too often to debating the school lunch menu, arguing about frustrating co-workers, or the crazy antics of various family members, then work to bring the discussion back around to how that applies to the key focus of the session for that meeting.
5. Draw out the quiet ones. Don't embarrass or push them to answer when they really don't feel comfortable, but work to create an environment where anyone can feel comfortable sharing an answer and giving an opinion. Give them space to answer when they are ready.
6. Remember you don't have to have all the answers. As the leader, many times people think that means they have to know all the answers to whatever questions may be asked. It's OK to say, "I don't know, what do you all think?" and get the opinions of the group. If no one knows, tell them you'll do some looking into the question and let them know at the next meeting. Seek the advice of your pastor or religious leader to help you if you get truly stumped.

Session Key Focus Points
This section is provided to give you, as the leader, an idea of the over-arching idea of each session. The questions within the session are designed to dig deeper, but this will give you a picture of where the session is headed so you can help guide the direction of the discussion.

Introduction
Even though this is a book in the Old Testament, it ties in beautifully with the New Testament and with Jesus's focus on how He managed His day and His time. This book focuses on priorities in our life. As we learn to prioritize our days in the same way as Jesus, we will have no regrets.

Session 1: Without Regrets
We all have reasons for why we do things. Very few things in our lives are truly spontaneous. Studying this book is one of them. As you look into why the book was written in the first place and the goal of the author, you can use that to clarify why you chose to study this book and what you hope to gain from the time spent studying it. Understanding Solomon can help shape our own understanding of ourselves.

Session 2: Everything is Meaningless
Most people have felt this way at some point in their lives. It's important to understand that it's OK to feel that way and that God can use that feeling in our lives to spur us on to more things. People who are completely content in their lives rarely put forth effort to change. Those who find themselves frustrated and unsatisfied are the ones who are willing to try things to change and to grow. Are you uncomfortable enough with the status quo that you are willing to do whatever is necessary to see change. Solomon was. Are you?

Session 3: Solomon's Experiments
As we get uncomfortable with our current situation, we may end up trying various things to improve our situation. Solomon did. Unfortunately, the things that he tried didn't work out as well as he had hoped. Are we willing to learn from his mistakes or do we walk the same path of "hard knocks" to learn? What do we expect from God as we are searching for the answers to our questions in life? Do we expect Him to answer us and work with us? Do we even ask Him our questions?

Session 4: Time and Justice
Sometimes, if we're not getting what we want, it's much easier to wait and expect others to just fix it for us. Solomon works through a couple of outside areas that he thinks might be able to give His life the meaning that He expected it to have. Instead of waiting on outside influences to impact our lives, we are to seek God and recognize that He is the answer to our questions in life.

Session 5: Power and Attitude
Power and attitude are two things that are essentially neutral, it's really about how we choose to use them in our lives. What is the impact of choosing to use these negatively? What about positively? Making the conscious choice to use these positively is very difficult. People often start out with the best of intentions, only to find themselves getting pulled to the negative more and more often. How can we keep ourselves focused on the positive?

Session 6: Life
How would you sum up your life to others? What is the legacy that you want to leave when you are gone? These are the core points that Solomon wrestles with in this chapter. If you don't like what you feel the answers are to those two questions above, what are you doing to change the answers?

While we are still living, there is still opportunity to change our legacy.

Session 7: Describing Wisdom
What does it mean to be truly wise? What advantage is there to being wise? As Solomon was the wisest man on earth, we can learn a lot from him on the subject of wisdom. Keeping our focus on the things that truly matter is a key component of wisdom.

Session 8: Applying Wisdom to Life
We've all known those people who were smart intellectually, but who didn't know or understand how to navigate common life situations. Wisdom is only as helpful as it is applied. How do you apply Godly wisdom in your life? How can you do so on a more consistent basis?

Session 9: Living to Die
Thinking back to the session on "Life," how would we rearrange our daily priorities if we knew exactly when we were going to die? This session really deals with the idea of living backwards. We know what our future holds, and that is death for this earthly body. So, if we are going to work backwards from that truth, how does that impact our decisions today?

Session 10: The Fool and His Reward
Being wise or being foolish doesn't only impact ourselves. Others that we are around are impacted by our wise or foolish choices. If we asked others to rate us on a scale of 1 to 10 based on our wisdom and foolishness, how would we rate? We must be accountable for the actions that we take, the impact those actions have on others, and whether we would have acted differently if we had more wisdom in that situation.

Session 11: Attitude Adjustment
We can follow through on all the things that have been learned in the previous sessions, but if that's done with the wrong attitude, then it doesn't matter. Our attitude toward everything that we come into contact with in life is a reflection of our relationship with Jesus Christ. What does that reflection look like when it is on display for others to see and experience?

Session 12: Enhance Your Memory
Knowing everything that you should do and yet not doing it, is the height of foolishness. Solomon knows that no matter what you heard or understood from all the lessons that he just taught through the book, if you don't take it to heart and remember to act on it, then it has done you no good. Don't waste the time spent learning these lessons. Commit them to memory and act on them daily.

Book of Ecclesiastes Outline

I. Solomon's introduction (1:1-18)

   A. Author and Thesis (1:1-2)

   B. Examples of thesis (1:3-11)

   1. Futility in Nature (1:3-7)

   2. Futility in Man (1:8-11)

   C. The Preacher's reason for his Thesis (1:12-18)

   1. He is driven to make the statement (1:12-13)

   2. He is qualified to make the statement (1:14-18)

II. Solomon's Experiments (2:1-26)

   A. He tried to find fulfillment in physical and material pleasure (2:1-11)

B. He tried to find fulfillment in excelling in wisdom (2:12-17)

C. He tried to find fulfillment in hard work (2:18-26)

1. Excelling at labor does not bring satisfaction (2:18-23)

2. Only God can give a person's actions meaning (2:24-26)

III. Solomon's Observations (3:1-6:12)

A. Time (3:1-15)

1. How time is proportioned on earth (3:1-9)

2. The complexity of eternity (3:10-11)

3. How God uses time and how we should respond (3:12-15)

B. Justice (3:16-22)

1. Man left to himself is unjust (3:16)

2. God is just and will judge man (3:17-18)

3. The fate of man will be the same as the beasts who are also created (3:19-22)

C. Power (4:1-16)

1. Oppression as a means of power (4:1-3)

2. Labor as a means of power (4:4-8)

3. Friendship as a means of power (4:9-12)

4. Wisdom as a means of power (4:13-16)

D. Attitudes (5:1-20)

1. Wrong attitudes toward God (5:1-10)

  2. Wrong attitudes toward possessions (5:11-20)

E. Life (6:1-12)

  1. Life has no meaning because wealth and all the things attained in life are meaningless (6:1-3)

  2. Life has no meaning because it can distract us from our focus on God (6:4-6)

  3. Life has no meaning because labor and all the things done in life are meaningless (6:7-12)

IV. Solomon's advice (7:1-10:20)

A. It is better to have wisdom than folly (7:1-8:17)

  1. Proverbs on Wisdom (7:1-14)

  2. Wisdom and Life (7:15-18)

    a. Wisdom does not extend life, so don't brag about it (7:15-16)

    b. Wickedness does not always shorten life, but folly might, so be careful (7:17-18)

  3. The characteristics of wisdom (7:19-29)

    a. Wisdom enables people to differentiate between the important and frivolous things in life (7:19-22)

    b. Wisdom cannot be attained by hard work and is not found in very many people (7:23-29)

  4. The Use of Wisdom (8:1-17)

                a. Using wisdom when dealing with those in authority (8:1-9)

                b. Using wisdom with wicked and righteous men (8:10-15)

                c. Using wisdom when dealing with God (8:16-17)

    B. We will all die someday (9:1-18)

        1. What should our attitude be? (9:1-9)

        2. What should our actions be? (9:10-19)

    C. Foolishness is detrimental to all (10:1-20)

        1. Foolishness and Wisdom: The Contrast (10:1-7)

        2. Foolishness and Wisdom: The Actions (10:8-15)

        3. Foolishness and Wisdom: The Effect on Others (10:16-20)

V. Solomon's Conclusions (11:1-12:14)

    A. Based on all this, what should our attitude be? (11:1-10)

        1. Our Attitude Toward Others (11:1-2)

        2. Our Attitude Toward the Future (11:3-5)

        3. Our Attitude Toward Work (11:6-7)

        4. Our Attitude Toward Life (11:8-10)

    B. Based on all this, what should we remember? (12:1-14)

        1. Remember your past (12:1-4)

        2. Remember your future (12:5-8)

3. Remember Truth (12:9-12)
4. Remember God (12:13-14)

About the Author

I never planned to be a writer. It's always interesting how God works and He has a way of bringing us right around to the place where He wants us. Several years ago, God led me through some difficult times in my personal life. Only by studying and applying the truths found in the Bible did I find the answers I needed to get life back on track and figure out how to follow God, no matter what.

Now, I continue to work daily to put these truths into practice. Some days are better than others, but by God's grace, I am making progress and I'm so happy He hasn't given up on me! I am passionate about studying and applying the God's Word into daily life and I invite others to share in the peace that can be found when you're choosing to follow God.

My husband, D Burchfiel, and our two amazing kids currently make our home in Wichita, KS

I'm around online several places, so please reach out and connect with me so we can share the journey together!

Website – www.kristiburchfiel.com
Twitter – @kristiburchfiel
Facebook Page – Without Regrets: A Study of Ecclesiastes

Other Books
Bible Studies:

The Decay Within: A Study of Amos
Without Regrets: A Study of Ecclesiastes
Piecing Together Forgiveness: A Study of Philemon

The Daily Devotional Series:
The Daily Devotional Series: Gospel of John
The Daily Devotional Series: Genesis
The Daily Devotional Series: Psalm volume 1
The Daily Devotional Series: Psalm volume 2
The Daily Devotional Series: Psalm volume 3
The Daily Devotional Series: 365 Devotions Through the New Testament
The Daily Devotional Series: 1 & 2 Chronicles
The Daily Devotional Series: Proverbs
The Daily Devotional Series: 1, 2, & 3 John
The Daily Devotional Series: Jeremiah

How to Become a Christian

We are all sinners
- Romans 3:23—for all have sinned and fall short of the glory of God
- Isaiah 53:6—We all, like sheep, have gone astray, each of us has turned to our own way; and the Lord has laid on him the iniquity of us all

The result of our sin is that we all deserve death
- Romans 6:23—For the wages of sin is death, but the free gift of God is eternal life in Christ Jesus our Lord.
- God paid the penalty for our sins on our behalf through the death of his Son, Jesus Christ
- Romans 5:8—But God demonstrates His own love toward us, in that while we were yet sinners, Christ died for us.
- 1 Peter 3:18—For Christ also suffered once for sins, the righteous for the unrighteous, to bring you to God.

He was put to death in the body but made alive in the Spirit.

When we acknowledge our sin and understand God's free gift of salvation, accept God's gift and allow Him to be Lord of our life, he saves us.
- Romans 10:9-10, 13—that if you confess with your mouth Jesus as Lord, and believe in your heart that God raised Him from the dead, you will be saved; for with the heart a person believes, resulting in righteousness, and with the mouth he confesses, resulting in salvation. For whoever will call on the name of the Lord will be saved.

Admit that you are a sinner, believe that God has provided a way through Jesus for you to be saved, and confess or pray to God and ask Him to be the Lord of your life. He loves you!
- John 1:12—But as many as received Him, to them He gave the right to become the children of God, even to those who believe in His name.
- John 17:3—Now this is eternal life; that they may know you, the only true God, and Jesus Christ, whom you have sent.

If you make a decision to follow Jesus Christ as your Lord and Savior, I would love to hear about it! Please send me an email at kristi@kristiburchfiel.com and let me know!

Bonus Book – The Daily Devotional Series: Gospel of John

Introduction
What is The Daily Devotional Series?
The Daily Devotional Series was born from my own personal devotions. As part of my daily time with God, I wanted to be able to read and study a whole book of the Bible at a time. However, I also wanted to be able to focus on one specific thought or idea that I could hold on to for the whole day.

Ultimately, I decided to take one book of the Bible at a time, read through one chapter a day, and then focus on a truth from one verse in that chapter. This allows me to balance the consistency of going through a whole book at a time with the specific focus I need for that particular day.

How do I use The Daily Devotional Series?
I encourage you to take the time to read through the entire chapter for each day so you can get the full story and background information. However, realize that is not necessary to be able to follow and learn from the devotionals. Each devotional focuses on one verse, the truth in that verse, and a response to pray back to God.

Because of this format, there will be verses and ideas that are not focused on. This is not an exhaustive study of each of these books, just a nugget of truth from each chapter. I encourage you to find time to balance your studies by also spending some time studying each the book as a whole. For a more comprehensive look through a book in the Bible, check out my Bible Studies listed at the end of this book.

May you be blessed as you study God's word and apply it to your life daily.

Background

The Gospel of John is one of four Biblical accounts of the life and works of Jesus. The author, John, was one of Jesus' twelve disciples and started out being known as one of the "Sons of Thunder" along with his brother James.

However, through his encounter with Jesus, John came to understand what it meant to truly love others. John experienced such a life-altering change that, instead of being a "Son of Thunder," he refers to himself as the "disciple whom Jesus loved." John's passion for Jesus Christ and his desire to share Christ's love motivated him to write his first-hand knowledge of what He experienced and learned in his time with Jesus Christ, Son of God.

John lived the longest of the twelve disciples after the resurrection of Jesus. He probably wrote this book first, but he also wrote several other books of the Bible, including 1, 2, and 3 John and the book of Revelation. More than likely, out of the four Gospel accounts (Matthew, Mark, and Luke), John was written last, and contains several passages that are unique to this Gospel alone.

John's focus in writing this book is very clearly to present an argument that Jesus Christ is the Son of God, the one true Messiah, and the only way for people to receive the gift of eternal life. John clearly spells out the fact that Jesus is God throughout his writings and challenges his readers to make a choice to believe and follow Jesus Christ.

The clear language and compelling stories and truths found in the Gospel of John have made this a favorite of preachers, evangelists, disciples, and seekers of truth ever since it was written. May your life be touched and as you read through one truth from each chapter and ask God to apply it to your life.

*****

Chapter 1

John 1:17—For the Law was given through Moses; grace and truth were realized through Jesus Christ.

Truth:
Moses was given the Law to allow us to see God's standard of perfection. If we compare ourselves to the law, none of us measure up. Jesus Christ came in truth; the truth that allowed Him to fulfill God's standard of perfection. He also came in grace; the grace that offers to share that truth with those of us who would submit our lives to Him.

Response:
Lord, Your grace is amazing and Your truth is perfection. Thank You for taking my imperfection and giving me Your grace!

*****

Chapter 2

John 2:5—His mother said to the servants, "Whatever He says to you, do it."

Truth:
In this circumstance, Mary knew that Jesus would have the answer, but it might not make sense to the servants. Jesus has the answer to every one of our circumstances, but the answers don't always make sense to us at first. Do we trust Him enough to do whatever He says to do?

Response:
Lord, I don't need to have all the answers. Help me trust and do all that You have for me to do.

*****

Chapter 3
John 3:36—He who believes in the Son has eternal life, but he who does not obey the Son will not see life, but the wrath of God abides on him.

Truth:
God's Son Jesus makes the way for us to receive the gift of eternal life. The Lord is very clear that this is the only way to receive this gift. If someone does not believe and obey, then they have God's wrath. Have we received this gift? Have we shared it with others?

Response:
Lord, thank You for Your amazing gift! Help me to share this amazing gift with everyone I meet.

*****

Chapter 4
John 4:42—and they were saying to the woman, "it is no longer because of what you said that we believe, for we have heard for ourselves and know that this One is indeed the Savior of the world."

Truth:
Each person, regardless of how they first heard of Jesus Christ, must eventually have a personal encounter with Him and see Christ for who He is. The testimony of others is important for it draws us to God in the first place. However, the decision to follow Him is ours alone. Have we made a personal decision to follow Christ?

Response:
Lord, thank you for wonderful people who told me of You. Thank You for showing Yourself to me more and more each day as I personally trust in You.

*****

Chapter 5
John 5:19—Therefore Jesus answered and was saying to them, "Truly, truly I say to you, the Son can do nothing of Himself unless it is something He sees the Father doing, for whatever the Father does, these things the Son also does in like manner."

Truth:
Jesus is God, yet He states that He can do nothing but what God the Father has for Him. If Jesus can do nothing without God, how much more does that apply to us! Do we allow Jesus to live through us so that everything we do is done by God?

Response:
Lord, take my life. Help me to decrease and for You to increase so that I, too, do nothing of myself.

*****

Chapter 6
John 6:6—This He was saying to test him for He Himself knew what He was intending to do.

Truth:
When we're confronted with crisis, God offers us the opportunity to trust Him and have faith. In this situation, and in all others, Jesus knew what He was going to do, but He gave the disciples an opportunity to trust in Him and grow in their relationship with Him.

Response:
Lord, help me to trust You even through the hard times when I don't see an answer. I know You already know what You are intending to do.

*****

Chapter 7

John 7:18—He who speaks for himself seeks his own glory, but he who is seeking the glory of the One who sent Him, He is true and there is no unrighteousness in Him.

Truth:
When we speak, our words reveal a lot about ourselves and our motives. If we are seeking God's will and His glory, then our words will be a direct reflection of those motives. If not, then our words will betray us.

Response:
Lord, I pray that You will help me surrender any motives that are not glorifying to You, then allow me to speak the words that praise and exalt You.

*****

Chapter 8

John 8:12—Then Jesus again spoke to them saying "I am the Light of the world; he who follows me will not walk in the darkness but will have the Light of Life."

Truth:
Jesus is the light. Not just any light, the Light of Life. Do we feel like we are stumbling around in darkness throughout our day? Follow the Light in all that we do!

Response:
Lord, You bring Light to the path. Help me to follow You step by step along Your way.

*****

Chapter 9
John 9:25—He then answered, "Whether He is a sinner I do not know; one thing I do know, that though I was blind now I see."

Truth:
This man had been healed by Jesus and was called to give an account of what happened. Witnessing is simply about sharing our experience with Jesus Christ. When God works in our lives, do we share what has happened with those we are around?

Response:
Lord, thank You for the witness of this man. Thank You for working in my life; I give You all praise!

*****

Chapter 10
John 10:10—The thief comes to steal and kill and destroy. I come that they may have life and have it abundantly.

Truth:
Why did Jesus come? He came to give us life and allow us to have it abundantly. The Creator of life came to help us know what life really is. The thief wants to steal this from us. Do we accept the gift of abundant life or do we allow the thief to steal it from us?

Response:
Lord, fill me with Your abundant life as I surrender my life to You.

*****

Chapter 11
John 11:25—Jesus said to her, "I am the resurrection and the life; he who believes in Me will live even if he dies."
Truth:
Jesus speaks at this difficult time in their lives to help them understand that He is in control, even of the things that people have no control over like death. Do we trust Him to have the control in all the areas of our life?

Response:
Lord, thank You for being in control and being trustworthy in all areas of life! Thank You for being over all, including death!

*****

Chapter 12
Johns 12:43—for they loved the approval of men rather than the approval of God.

Truth:
People who believed in Jesus did not share their faith because they were afraid of what might happen to them. The Bible lists this as their reason. Do we use the same reasoning for the things we do or don't do? Are we actively seeking the approval of God or just settling for the approval of men?

Response:
Lord, help me to be actively seeking Your approval regardless of how other people respond.

*****

Chapter 13
John 13:35—by this all men will know that you are My disciples, if you have love for one another.

Truth:
The love and care that we show others is a key trait of followers of Jesus. When people look at our lives, do they see Jesus? Do they see Jesus' love displayed to others?

Response:
Lord, I pray my life will testify to You today by the love and care that I show others.

*****

Chapter 14
John 14:6—Jesus said to him "I am the way and the truth and the life; no one comes to the Father but through Me."

Truth:
Jesus is the key. He is the only One through whom we have access to God. He is the Way. He is the Truth. He alone is the Life. He makes it possible for us in our sin and brokenness to come to the Father, the Creator of all things, and be made His child.

Response:
Father thank you for giving us a perfect Way, perfect Truth, and perfect Life.

*****

Chapter 15
John 15:12—This is my commandment that you love one another, just as I have loved you.

Truth:
Love is a commandment. We are to love; not just any love, but love as Jesus loves. We cannot do this alone, but only by Jesus who loves through us. Do we love as Jesus loves us?

Response:
Lord, I want to follow Your command. Help me love as You love!

*****

Chapter 16
John 16:33—These things I have spoken to you so that in Me you may have peace. In the world you have tribulation but take courage; I have overcome the world.

Truth:
What encouragement! Jesus Christ has overcome the world and He reminds us of the peace, courage, and hope that we have through Him. Whatever we are going through now, Jesus has overcome!

Response:
Lord, thank You for overcoming and giving peace and hope through You!

*****

Chapter 17
John 17:15—I do not ask to take them out of the world, but to keep them from the evil one.

Truth:
Jesus prayed for his disciples. He doesn't ask that they avoid problems all together, but that they avoid the evil one. We are going to have difficulties in this world; Jesus is not taking us away from the hard times. But, He will help us avoid the temptation to sin while in the midst of them.

Response:
Lord, help me to seek You through the tough times, knowing that You are there and will help me go through them without being distracted by the evil one.

*****

Chapter 18
John 18:11—So Jesus said to Peter, "Put the sword into the sheath; the cup which the Father has given Me, shall I not drink it?"

Truth:
God shares with us plans He has for us and we have the option to fight against those plans or to allow those plans to become part of us. Will we "drink the cup" of plans that God has for us or try to fight against God's plan?

Response:
Jesus, since You can drink Your cup, help me to drink the cups that You have for me, so that I may always follow Your will for my life.

*****

Chapter 19
John 19:30b—He said, "It is finished!" and he bowed his head and gave up His spirit.

Truth:
The Lord Jesus Christ finished everything here that the Father had for Him to do. That is when He was able to voluntarily give up His spirit and complete the sacrifice that He made on our behalf.

Response:
Lord, thank You for the sacrifice that made it possible for me to be in a relationship with You.

*****

Chapter 20
John 20:21—So Jesus said to them again, "Peace be with you; as the Father has sent Me, I also send you."

Truth:
The idea of being sent out like Jesus was sent out can cause some anxiety, and yet Jesus tells us to have peace. In truth, we only find peace in being exactly where God has for us to be, doing what God has for us to do.

Response:
Father, I pray that I go when and where You send me, and that I will rest in Your peace.

*****

Chapter 21
John 21:22—Jesus said to him, "If I want him to remain until I come, what is that to you? You follow Me!"

Truth:
It can be easy to get focused on other people and what God has planned for their lives. However, we should not allow God's plans for others to distract us from what God has planned in our own lives. Will we follow God regardless of what other people are called to do?

Response:
Lord, help me to focus on You and follow You regardless of Your plans for the others I'm around.

Thanks for reading! *The Daily Devotional Series: Gospel of John* is available as an ebook for FREE from all major ebook suppliers. This short devotional style book is one of several devotional books that take the reader through a verse that is a key point of focus, a truth about that verse, and then a prayer of response. Please check out the other Daily Devotional Series Books available in ebook and paperback from your favorite book retailer.

www.ingramcontent.com/pod-product-compliance
Lightning Source LLC
Chambersburg PA
CBHW072041290426
44110CB00014B/1551